Elements in Philosophy and Logic
edited by
Bradley Armour-Garb
*SUNY Albany*
Frederick Kroon
*The University of Auckland*

# THE LOGIC OF GROUNDING

Fabrice Correia
*University of Geneva*

Shaftesbury Road, Cambridge CB2 8EA, United Kingdom

One Liberty Plaza, 20th Floor, New York, NY 10006, USA

477 Williamstown Road, Port Melbourne, VIC 3207, Australia

314–321, 3rd Floor, Plot 3, Splendor Forum, Jasola District Centre,
New Delhi – 110025, India

103 Penang Road, #05–06/07, Visioncrest Commercial, Singapore 238467

Cambridge University Press is part of Cambridge University Press & Assessment, a department of the University of Cambridge.

We share the University's mission to contribute to society through the pursuit of education, learning and research at the highest international levels of excellence.

www.cambridge.org
Information on this title: www.cambridge.org/9781009547802

DOI: 10.1017/9781009180504

© Fabrice Correia 2024

This publication is in copyright. Subject to statutory exception and to the provisions of relevant collective licensing agreements, no reproduction of any part may take place without the written permission of Cambridge University Press & Assessment.

When citing this work, please include a reference to the DOI 10.1017/9781009180504

First published 2024

*A catalogue record for this publication is available from the British Library.*

ISBN 978-1-009-54780-2 Hardback
ISBN 978-1-009-18051-1 Paperback
ISSN 2516-418X (online)
ISSN 2516-4171 (print)

Cambridge University Press & Assessment has no responsibility for the persistence or accuracy of URLs for external or third-party internet websites referred to in this publication and does not guarantee that any content on such websites is, or will remain, accurate or appropriate.

# The Logic of Grounding

Elements in Philosophy and Logic

DOI: 10.1017/9781009180504
First published online: October 2024

Fabrice Correia
*University of Geneva*

**Author for correspondence:** Fabrice Correia, fabrice.correia@unige.ch

**Abstract:** The concept of grounding – of a fact obtaining in virtue of other facts – has been a topic of intensive philosophical and logical investigation over roughly the past two decades. Many philosophers take grounding to deserve a central place in metaphysical theorizing, in great part because it is thought to do a better job than other concepts – for example, reduction and supervenience – at capturing certain phenomena. Studies on the logic of grounding have largely been conducted with this philosophical background in mind. In this Element, the author tries to give a faithful picture of the contemporary development of the logic of grounding in a way that is both reasonably comprehensive and reasonably systematic.

**Keywords:** logic of grounding, metaphysical grounding, metaphysical explanation, metaphysical equivalence, puzzles of grounding

© Fabrice Correia 2024

ISBNs: 9781009547802 (HB), 9781009180511 (PB), 9781009180504 (OC)
ISSNs: 2516-418X (online), 2516-4171 (print)

# Contents

| | | |
|---|---|---:|
| | Introduction | 1 |
| 1 | The Jungle of Grounding | 2 |
| 2 | Pure Logics | 7 |
| 3 | Impure Logics | 28 |
| 4 | Further Topics | 60 |
| | Appendix: Labelled Trees | 79 |
| | References | 83 |

## Introduction

Although the concept of grounding has been widely used throughout the history of western philosophy (see Raven 2020, part I), it has almost never been a proper topic of investigation until the beginning of the twenty-first century. Bolzano (1837) is a significant counterexample – to my knowledge, the only one – to the claim that grounding has *never* up to that period been a proper topic of investigation (see Roski and Schnieder 2022). The starting point of current theorizing about grounding can be traced back to the works of Fine (2001, 2010, 2012a, 2012b), Correia (2005, 2010), Schaffer (2009, 2010), Rosen (2010) and Schnieder (2010, 2011).

The topic of this Element – the *logic* of grounding – is part and parcel of the study of grounding, just like modal logic is part and parcel of the study of necessity and possibility and tense logic is part and parcel of the study of the concepts of past, present and future.

The logic of grounding does not have the grandiose pedigree of modal logic and tense logic, and it has achieved much less than them. One sometimes hears sceptical complaints against the very concept of grounding based precisely on the fact that the logic of grounding is not even close to its venerable cousins in terms of systematicity and other theoretical virtues. But it should not be surprising that logical theorizing about grounding is in the state it currently is, for two reasons. The first one is that – leaving (again) Bolzano aside – work on the logic of grounding is very recent: the first published works on the topic are from 2010. Bear in mind that about 50 years elapsed from the impetus of C. I. Lewis's work on modal logic to the beauties of Kripke-style semantics, at a time when there was not shortage of talented logicians. The second reason is that grounding is, unlike modal and tense-logical notions as standardly understood, *hyperintensional* rather than 'merely intensional'. Kripke-style semantics is a wonderful tool to model intensional notions. We do not have comparable tools to handle hyperintensionality. Hyperintensional notions, such as grounding and (plausibly) essence, knowledge, obligation and many others, are notoriously very difficult to handle in a satisfactory way.

In what follows, I try to give a faithful picture of the development of the logic of grounding over the twelve years or so preceding the writing of this Element, in a way that is at the same time reasonably comprehensive and reasonably systematic. Due to space limitation, some sacrifices had to be made in both respects – I explicitly mention some of them in due course – but hopefully they are not too many or too significant.

The plan is as follows. Section 1 introduces the notion of grounding in its multiple variants or species. Sections 2 and 3 deal with the logic of grounding, the 'pure' logic and the 'impure' logic, respectively. Section 4 is devoted to two further topics: the theory of ground-theoretic equivalence and cognate notions and the puzzles of grounding.

# 1 The Jungle of Grounding

A great number of notions of grounding have been distinguished in the literature, and different logics of grounding often target different such notions. In this section, I try to give a reasonably comprehensive survey of these notions.

## 1.1 The Canonical Notion of Grounding

Let me start with what I will dub *the canonical notion of grounding*. This is the notion that has been most studied and used by philosophers and logicians in the past dozen years.

The notion is often expressed by means of predicates of facts, as in the following sentence type:

(1) The fact that $q$, the fact that $r$, ... ground the fact that $p$

Alternatively, one may express the notion using sentential operators as in:

(2) $p$ because $q, r, \ldots$
(3) Its being the case that $q$, that $r$, ... make it the case that $p$

One also encounters hybrid expressions, partly operational and partly predicational, such as:

(4) $p$ in virtue of the fact that $q$, the fact that $r$, ...

These modes of expression are, of course, far from being equivalent from the point of view of logical grammar. Only if grounding is expressed by means of a predicate as in (1) can it be properly said to be a *relation*. However, for ease of expression it is often convenient to speak as if grounding were a relation even on the assumption that it is expressed by means of a sentential operator or a hybrid expression. I will feel free to do that in what follows.

The canonical notion of grounding has the following three features: it is (i) *(one or many)-to-one*, (ii) *factive* and (iii) *metaphysical*. In order to spell this out, let me first adopt the predicational mode of formulation.

To say that a notion of grounding is (one or many)-to-one is to say that grounding of the corresponding sort is always of one particular fact, and that when a fact is grounded, it may be grounded in one fact, or in several facts taken together without being grounded in each of these facts taken individually. This aspect of the canonical notion is made syntactically explicit in (1) by having a list of fact-terms on the left of the predicate – which may contain only one element – and a single fact-term on the right. The view that there are (one or many)-to-one relations is far from being heretical: causation and (the intuitive notion of) logical consequence are arguably of that kind.

To say that a notion of grounding is *factive* is to say that grounding of the corresponding sort relates facts. This aspect of the canonical notion is also made explicit in (1) by the choice of the terms that flank the predicate. Facts, in this context, may be understood as *obtaining* states of affairs, or alternatively as *true* propositions.

There are two main ways of cashing out the idea that the canonical notion of grounding is *metaphysical*. One is to say that it is metaphysical insofar as it entails *metaphysical necessitation* – that is, insofar as the following conditional holds[1]:

(Nec) If some facts $G, H, \ldots$ ground a fact $F$ in the canonical sense, then as a matter of metaphysical necessity, if $G, H, \ldots$ all obtain, then $F$ also obtains.

Despite its popularity, this principle has been criticized (see Leuenberger 2014 and Skiles 2015). The other main way of cashing out the idea is in terms of *comparative fundamentality*. On that account, the canonical notion is metaphysical insofar as the following holds[2]:

(Fund) If some facts $G, H, \ldots$ ground a fact $F$ in the canonical sense, then each of $G, H, \ldots$ is more fundamental than $F$.

Fundamentality here is of course to be understood as metaphysical fundamentality, as opposed to, say, epistemic fundamentality.[3] Note that these two ways of cashing out the metaphysical character of grounding may be orthogonal: it does not seem to be incoherent to hold that some notions of grounding satisfy (Nec) but not (Fund) and that some notions of grounding (leaving aside 'partial' notions, see below) satisfy (Fund) but not (Nec). I propose a disjunctive account of metaphysicality: for a notion of grounding to be metaphysical is for it to satisfy (Nec) or (Fund) or both.

Importantly, the fact that the canonical notion of grounding is metaphysical does not preclude there being cases of grounding in the canonical sense that are 'logical' or 'conceptual'. Compare (5) and (6) below with (7)–(10):

(5) Mental facts are grounded in physical facts

---

[1] Fine (2012a), among many others, accepts this conditional.
[2] Bennett (2011, 2017), among many others, accepts this conditional.
[3] Metaphysical fundamentality can in turn be understood in various ways. Bennett (2017) makes the point very clear.

(6) The existence of a whole is grounded in the existence of its parts

(7) The fact that it is both raining and cold is grounded in the fact that it is raining and the fact that it is cold

(8) The fact that 2 + 2 = 4 or 1 = 0 is grounded in the fact that 2 + 2 = 4

(9) The fact that John is a bachelor is grounded in the fact that he is an adult, the fact that he is a male and the fact that he is not married

(10) The fact that the sky is coloured is grounded in the fact that it is blue

(5)–(10) are all typical claims involving the canonical notion. In all these cases, what grounds plausibly metaphysically necessitates what is grounded. But in (7)–(10) the link between the grounds and the groundees is not *merely* one of metaphysical necessitation: it is arguably one of *conceptual* necessitation; and in the case of (7) and (8) it is also arguably one of *logical* necessitation.

I have spelled out the three features of the canonical notion of grounding – being (one or many)-to-one, being factive and being metaphysical – on the assumption that the notion is expressed by means of a predicate as in (1) above. Assuming instead that the canonical notion is expressed by means of a sentential operator – say, 'because' – only requires a few adjustments. The canonical notion is *(one or many)-to-one* insofar as the basic claims involving it are of the form (2), where what is on the right-hand side of 'because' may comprise one or more items. The notion is *factive* insofar as for all $p, q, r, \ldots$, if $p$ because $q, r, \ldots$, then $p, q, r, \ldots$. The notion is *metaphysical* insofar as it satisfies at least one of the following two conditions:

(Nec*) For all $p, q, r, \ldots$, if $p$ because $q, r, \ldots$, then as a matter of metaphysical necessity, if $q, r, \ldots$, then $p$

(Fund*) For all $p, q, r, \ldots$, if $p$ because $q, r, \ldots$, then its being the case that $q$ is more fundamental than its being the case that $p$, its being the case that $r$ is more fundamental than its being the case that $p, \ldots$

It should be clear how the three features are to be spelled out on the assumption that the canonical notion of grounding is expressed by means of a hybrid expression.

A further feature of the canonical notion of grounding is that it is *explanatory*. Two quite different ways of cashing this out have been put forward in the literature: there is on one hand the view that grounding *is* a form of explanation; and there is on the other hand the view that grounding is not a form of explanation but is rather, like causation, a determinative notion that *backs* explanations (see Raven 2015 for a discussion and relevant references). On both views, the type of explanation involved is taken to be distinctively metaphysical (on metaphysical explanation, see Brenner et al. 2021).

On the assumption that the canonical notion of grounding is explanatory, one may argue that it is both *relevant* and *non-monotonic*. Assuming that the notion is expressed by means of a predicate (here as in many other places throughout this Element, I will leave the other modes of expression aside for the sake of brevity), these features can be glossed as follows: the notion is relevant in the sense that when some facts ground a further fact, each of the former facts is relevant to the obtaining of the grounded fact; and it is non-monotonic in the sense that from the hypothesis that a fact $F$ is grounded in some facts $G, H, \ldots$, one cannot validly infer that $F$ is grounded in $G, H, \ldots$ together with other arbitrary facts. (Note that non-monotonicity arguably follows from relevance.) In both respects, the canonical notion of grounding differs from classical logical consequence. Relevance and non-monotonicity are features that are often attributed to the canonical notion of grounding, often independently from their connection with explanatoriness.

## 1.2 Other Notions

The other notions of grounding that have been discussed or simply mentioned in the literature depart from the canonical notion in one or more features of the latter. Let me run through the relevant features in turn, starting with some features that have been discussed in the previous section:

*Being (one or many)-to-one.* Some authors have taken seriously the idea that there can be cases of 'zero-grounding', that is, (speaking in the predicational mode) cases of metaphysical strict full grounding where the ground is the empty collection of facts rather than a collection of one or more facts (see for instance Fine 2012a and Litland 2017). And some authors have argued that there can be cases where a plurality of facts is metaphysically strictly fully grounded which cannot be reduced to cases in which the members of the plurality are individually grounded (see for instance Dasgupta 2014 and Litland 2016).

*Being factive.* Several authors countenance notions of grounding that are not factive (see for instance Correia 2014, 2017; Fine 2012a and Litland 2017).

*Being metaphysical.* The literature on grounding features, alongside metaphysical grounding, notions of grounding of other kinds, like *logical* grounding, *conceptual* grounding, *natural* grounding or again *normative* grounding (see for instance Correia 2005, 2014 and Fine 2012a).

In addition to having the features mentioned in the previous section, the canonical notion is both *full* and *strict* (the vocabulary of 'full' versus 'partial' and 'strict' versus 'weak' is from Fine 2012a). The canonical notion is full insofar as the grounds, in the canonical sense, of a fact are sufficient for the fact to obtain. And it is strict insofar as it is, strictly speaking, a notion of 'making the case' or 'obtaining in virtue of'. Fine (2012a) ties the notion of strictness with that of irreflexivity or non-circularity: he takes it that no fact can strictly ground, or even help strictly ground, itself. This may be true; but if it is, it is a substantial, non-analytic truth.[4] Other notions of grounding discussed in the literature lack one or both of these features:

*Being full.* Fine (2012a) introduces notions of grounding that are *partial*, that is, not full. Here is the definition of one of them: $G$ partially grounds $F$ iff$_{df}$ $F$ is grounded in the canonical sense in $G$, or in $G$ together with other facts. (Note that even though the *notion* just defined is not full, given the definition every full ground, in the canonical sense of 'ground', is a partial ground.)

*Being strict.* Fine (2012a) also introduces notions of grounding that are *weak*, that is, not strict. They are all reflexive. One can easily define such a notion in terms of the canonical notion: $G, H, \ldots$ weakly ground $F$ iff$_{df}$ either $G, H, \ldots$ ground in the canonical sense $F$, or $F$ is one of $G, H, \ldots$. (I hasten to stress that Fine 2012a does *not* propose such a definition.)

The five dimensions of departure from features of the canonical notion that have been discussed so far are prima facie independent from one another. Even if this first impression is incorrect, there are certainly sufficiently many independencies among these dimensions to already generate an impressive number of different notions of grounding – not all of which have been explicitly discussed or even just mentioned in the literature.

Let me close this section with a further distinction that adds even more to this variety. This is the distinction between *immediate* and *mediate* grounding (Fine 2012a). Fine illustrates the distinction as follows: the fact that $q \wedge r$ is immediately grounded in the fact that $q$ and the fact that $r$ (taken together), he claims, whereas the fact that $p \wedge (q \wedge r)$ is only mediately grounded in the fact that $p$, the fact that $q$ and the fact that $r$ (taken together). The canonical notion of grounding is certainly not an immediate notion. Fine holds that it should be identified with a mediate notion. In fact, he intends his example to feature the canonical notion and the corresponding immediate notion. Fine's view that the canonical notion should be identified with a mediate notion is a substantial view, at least if it is granted, as it seems reasonable to hold, that a mediate notion

---

[4] Compare with causation: whereas it may be true that causation, understood in the strict sense, is irreflexive, the view that there are cases of self-causation, understood strictly, is not incoherent.

must be definable in terms of chains of a corresponding immediate notion (I will come back to this at the end of Section 2.3).

## 2 Pure Logics

Following established terminology, I call a logic of grounding *pure* if it only deals with the structural properties of grounding, that is, the properties that grounding has irrespective of the logical structure of the grounds and the groundees. The studies discussed in Section 2.5 are purely proof-theoretic. Those discussed in the previous sections put forward semantics for the logic of grounding, some together with corresponding sound and complete proof systems. These semantics are of two kinds. Fine (2012b) (discussed in Section 2.1) invokes what is often called a 'truthmaker semantics'. deRosset (2014) (discussed in Section 2.2) and Litland (2016) (discussed in Section 2.4) also put forward such semantics. The remaining studies – deRosset (2015) and Litland (2018a) (discussed in Sections 2.3 and 2.4, respectively) – invoke graph-/tree-theoretic semantics.

### 2.1 Fine's 'The Pure Logic of Ground'

Fine's pure logic of grounding has four primitive operators:

$\leqslant$ expresses *weak full* grounding
$\preccurlyeq$ expresses *weak partial* grounding
$<$ expresses *strict full* grounding
$\prec$ expresses *strict partial* grounding

The language in which the logic is formulated has a given non-empty set of *basic sentences* which, from the point of view of the language, are simple, and the *sequents* of the language are all the expressions of the following types, where $\Delta$ is a (possibly empty) set of basic sentences and $\phi$ and $\psi$ are basic sentences:

(1) $\Delta \leqslant \phi$
(2) $\phi \preccurlyeq \psi$
(3) $\Delta < \phi$
(4) $\phi \prec \psi$

For the sake of homogeneity, it would be better to have either (2) and (4) of the form $\{\phi\} \preccurlyeq \psi$ and $\{\phi\} \prec \psi$, respectively, or alternatively to take $\Delta$ in (1) and (3) to be a plurality of sentences, as long as one allows empty pluralities and pluralities comprising only one item – but I will leave this detail aside.

Fine takes his ground-theoretic notions to be factive. But nothing in the logic he puts forward forces this interpretation of these notions, and it turns out that interpreting these notions as being non-factive is the most natural option.[5] Similarly, the ground-theoretic notions discussed in Sections 2.1 to 2.4 are all most naturally understood as being non-factive.

Fine does not say whether his notions are metaphysical (as opposed to, say, normative or natural), and so we may assume that the logic is intended to be neutral on the question. If $<$ is interpreted as expressing a metaphysical notion, $\Delta < \phi$ with $\Delta$ non-empty can be interpreted as the claim that the members of $\Delta$ ground, *in the canonical sense*, $\phi$.

On Fine's view, the four notions are intimately connected. Indeed, as this will be reflected in the logic, Fine takes $\leqslant$ to be the basic grounding relation in terms of which the other three notions are defined. Assuming that the language is suitably enriched, the definitions could be formulated as follows:

$$\phi \preccurlyeq \psi := \exists \Delta (\phi \in \Delta \wedge \Delta \leqslant \psi)$$
$$\phi < \psi := \phi \preccurlyeq \psi \wedge \neg (\psi \preccurlyeq \phi)$$
$$\Delta < \phi := \Delta \leqslant \phi \wedge \neg \exists \psi (\psi \in \Delta \wedge \phi \preccurlyeq \psi)$$

Fine discusses another notion of partial grounding, *partial strict grounding*, which he symbolizes as $\prec^*$ and which can be defined as follows:

$$\phi \prec^* \psi := \exists \Delta (\phi \in \Delta \wedge \Delta < \psi)$$

Importantly, partial strict grounding is *not* strict partial grounding (in Fine's logic, it can be shown that the former entails the latter and that the converse entailment fails), and Fine's pure logic of grounding features the latter notion, not the former.

Fine's system for the pure logic of grounding, PLG, is based on a list of rules of inference, where each rule says (or is to be interpreted as saying) that from a collection of 0 or more sequents (possibly infinitely many), one can infer a given sequent. The rules are listed in Figure 1.[6] Despite appearances,

---

[5] Anticipating a bit, every sequent of type $\phi \leqslant \phi$ is deemed a logical truth in Fine's logic. Since the basic sentences have no logical complexity, this is compatible with holding that $\leqslant$ is factive: we may simply stipulate that on their intended interpretation, the basic sentences are all true. But in interesting extensions of the logic, such as the extension I will present in Section 3.1, the basic sentences comprise sentences of type (say) $\psi \wedge \neg \psi$, and in such extensions the factive interpretation of $\leqslant$ is therefore ruled out (barring an extreme form of dialetheism). Given the definitional connections between $\leqslant$ and Fine's other grounding relations, if $\leqslant$ is understood as non-factive, then so should also be the other relations.

[6] Following common usage, I often use commas instead of set-theoretic union signs and drop set-theoretic brackets. Thus, $\Delta_1, \Delta_2, \ldots$ may be used for $\Delta_1 \cup \Delta_2 \cup \ldots$, $\Delta, \phi$ for $\Delta \cup \{\phi\}$ and $\phi_1, \phi_2, \ldots$ for $\{\phi_1\} \cup \{\phi_2\} \cup \ldots$. Caveat: the use of integer indices in the formulation of Cut ($\leqslant$) and Reverse Subsumption – as well as in the formulation of other rules that will be

## The Logic of Grounding

$$\frac{\Delta < \phi}{\Delta \leqslant \phi} \qquad \frac{\phi < \psi}{\phi \preccurlyeq \psi} \qquad \frac{\Delta, \phi < \psi}{\phi \prec \psi} \qquad \frac{\Delta, \phi \leqslant \psi}{\phi \preccurlyeq \psi} \qquad \text{Subsumption}$$

$$\frac{\Delta_1 \leqslant \phi_1 \quad \Delta_2 \leqslant \phi_2 \quad \ldots \quad \phi_1, \phi_2, \ldots \leqslant \phi}{\Delta_1, \Delta_2, \ldots \leqslant \phi} \qquad \text{Cut } (\leqslant)$$

$$\frac{\phi \preccurlyeq \psi \quad \psi \preccurlyeq \chi}{\phi \preccurlyeq \chi} \qquad \frac{\phi \preccurlyeq \psi \quad \psi < \chi}{\phi < \chi} \qquad \frac{\phi < \psi \quad \psi \preccurlyeq \chi}{\phi < \chi} \qquad \text{Transitivity}$$

$$\frac{}{\phi \leqslant \phi} \qquad \frac{\phi < \phi}{\bot} \qquad \text{Identity, Non-Circularity } (<)$$

$$\frac{\phi_1, \phi_2, \ldots \leqslant \phi \quad \phi_1 < \phi \quad \phi_2 < \phi \quad \ldots}{\phi_1, \phi_2, \ldots < \phi} \qquad \text{Reverse Subsumption}$$

**Figure 1** Rules for PLG

Non-Circularity ($<$) does not involve a special sequent $\bot$: the rule is meant to say that from any sequent of type $\phi < \phi$, any sequent can be inferred.

A sequent $\sigma$ is said to be *derivable* from a set $\Sigma$ of sequents in PLG iff $\sigma$ can be obtained from $\Sigma$ by means of the rules. Note that since PLG has some rules – namely, Cut ($\leqslant$) and Reverse Subsumption – that allow for infinitely many premisses, derivability cannot be formally defined in the familiar way in terms of *finite* sequences of items. But this can nevertheless be done in terms of sequences by saying that $\sigma$ is derivable from $\Sigma$ in PLG iff there is a (finite or infinite) sequence with a last member such that (i) $\sigma$ is the sequence's last member, and (ii) each member of the sequence is either a sequent in $\Sigma$, or an identity sequent $\phi \leqslant \phi$, or a sequent obtained from previous sequents by means of some rule distinct from Identity.[7] This is the way Fine goes. Another, somewhat more natural option invokes the notion of a labelled tree as defined in the Appendix: say that $\sigma$ is derivable from $\Sigma$ in PLG iff there is a tree with no infinite branch, labelled by sequents, such that (i) $\sigma$ is the tree's bottom, (ii) the tree's top contains only members of $\Sigma$ or sequents of type $\phi \leqslant \phi$, and (iii) for every parent node $n$ of the tree, there is (an instance of) a rule of inference

---

mentioned below, for that matter – is *not* meant to imply that the families of formulas or sets of formulas involved are denumerable.

[7] A sequence may have a last member and yet be infinite. Any sequence whose positions are isomorphic to the set of all ordinals smaller than or equal to $\omega$ (the first transfinite ordinal) endowed with the natural ordering is an illustration.

distinct from Identity whose conclusion labels $n$ and whose premises are the labels of $n$'s children.

A *derived rule* of the system is a rule of the same format as the previous rules whose conclusion is derivable from its premises in PLG. PLG has the following noteworthy derived rules:

$$\frac{\Delta_1 \leqslant \phi \quad \Delta_2 \leqslant \phi \quad \ldots}{\Delta_1, \Delta_2, \ldots \leqslant \phi} \quad \text{Amalgamation}(\leqslant)$$

$$\frac{\Delta_1 < \phi_1 \quad \Delta_2 < \phi_2 \quad \ldots \quad \phi_1, \phi_2, \ldots, \Gamma < \psi}{\Delta_1, \Delta_2, \ldots, \Gamma < \psi} \quad \text{Cut}(<)$$

$$\frac{\Delta, \phi < \phi}{\bot} \quad \text{Non-Circularity}(<)$$

$$\frac{\Delta_1 < \phi \quad \Delta_2 < \phi \quad \ldots}{\Delta_1, \Delta_2, \ldots < \phi} \quad \text{Amalgamation}(<)$$

Note the formal difference between Cut ($<$) and Cut ($\leqslant$): one gets Cut ($\leqslant$) from Cut ($<$) by substituting $\leqslant$ for $<$ and taking $\Gamma = \varnothing$. I will call the condition on $<$ expressed by Cut ($<$) *strong cut* and the condition on $\leqslant$ expressed by Cut ($\leqslant$) *weak cut*. It is easy to see that granted that $\leqslant$ satisfies weak cut and that Identity holds, $\leqslant$ also satisfies strong cut.

On the semantic side, the logic is characterized within Fine's general truth-maker semantical framework.[8] The framework's core semantic notion is that of *truthmaking* or *exact verification*. A truthmaker or exact verifier for a statement is wholly relevant to the truth of the statement. Fine contrasts exact verification with *inexact verification* and with *loose verification* – which Fine takes to be the notion standardly used in possible worlds semantics. An inexact verifier for a statement must be at least partly relevant to the truth of the statement, whereas a loose verifier for a statement is simply something that necessitates the truth of the statement and hence does not even need to be relevant to the truth of that statement. Trivially, any exact verifier is an inexact verifier. The view, upheld by Fine, that every inexact verifier is a loose verifier is plausible but substantial. To illustrate the three notions of verification, consider the state of my being both sitting and nervous. It exactly verifies the statement 'Fabrice is sitting and Fabrice is nervous', and it inexactly verifies 'Fabrice is sitting' without exactly verifying it. The same state loosely verifies the statement '$2 + 2 = 4$', but it fails to inexactly, and hence to exactly, verify it.

---

[8] See Fine (2017a, 2017b and 2017c).

## The Logic of Grounding

For the purpose of semantically characterizing PLG, Fine introduces what he calls 'generalized fact models', but which – in order to stick to the terminology he has come to adopt since then – I will call 'generalized *state* models'.

Let a *state frame* be a tuple $\langle S, \prod \rangle$ such that[9,10]:

- $S$ (states) is a non-empty set;
- $\prod$ (fusion) is an operation taking each subset of $S$ into a member of $S$, such that (i) for any $s \in S$, $\prod\{s\} = s$ and (ii) for any family $(S_i)_{i \in I}$ of subsets of $S$, $\prod\{\prod S_i : i \in I\} = \prod \bigcup_{i \in I} S_i$.

Instead of writing $\prod\{s_1, s_2, \ldots\}$ we may simply write $s_1 s_2 \ldots$ to improve readability. Say that a set of states $T$ in a state frame $\langle S, \prod \rangle$ is *closed* under $\prod$ iff for any non-empty subset $T^*$ of $T$, $\prod T^* \in T$. The *facts* of a state frame are the non-empty sets of states of that state frame that are closed under its fusion operation.[11] A *generalized state frame* is a tuple $\langle S, \prod, \mathcal{V} \rangle$, where $\langle S, \prod \rangle$ is a state frame and $\mathcal{V}$ (verification space) is a non-empty set of facts of $\langle S, \prod \rangle$. Finally, a *generalized state model* is defined as a tuple $\langle S, \prod, \mathcal{V}, [\,] \rangle$ where $\langle S, \prod, \mathcal{V} \rangle$ is a generalized state frame and $[\,]$ (verification valuation) is a function which takes each basic sentence of the language into a member of $\mathcal{V}$.

The fusion operation of a state frame is informally to be understood as conjunctive in nature, for example, as taking the state of my being sitting and the state of my being nervous into the state of my being both sitting and nervous. The verification space of a generalized state frame is thought of as the set of all the facts $F$ of the underlying state frame such that $F$ is capable of being the 'semantic value' of a statement, that is, the set of all the exact verifiers of a statement. Finally, where $\phi$ is a basic sentence and $[\,]$ the verification valuation of a generalized state model, $[\phi]$ – $\phi$'s *verification-set* – is accordingly thought of as the set of all the states that exactly verify $\phi$.

In order to interpret the sequents by means of generalized state models, it is useful to introduce a fusion operation on *sets of states* in addition to the

---

[9] In other papers, Fine works instead with *state spaces*, which are tuples $\langle S, \sqsubseteq \rangle$ where $S$ is a non-empty set and $\sqsubseteq$ a partial order on $S$, such that each subset of $S$ has a least upper bound for $\sqsubseteq$ in $S$. The two approaches are equivalent. To each state frame $\langle S, \prod \rangle$ there naturally corresponds the state space $\langle S, \sqsubseteq \rangle$ where $s \sqsubseteq t$ is stipulated to hold iff $t = \prod\{s, t\}$ (the structure can indeed be shown to be a state space given the properties of $\prod$); and to each state space $\langle S, \sqsubseteq \rangle$ there naturally corresponds the state frame $\langle S, \prod \rangle$ where $\prod T$ is stipulated to be $T$'s least upper bound for $\sqsubseteq$ in $S$ (the structure can indeed be shown to be a state frame given the properties of $\sqsubseteq$).

[10] I here follow Fine (2012b) and use '$\prod$' for state-fusion. The symbol is suggestive of the fact that state-fusion is conjunctive in character (see below). Elsewhere, Fine and others use '$\sqcup$' instead. I will later on use this latter symbol and variants thereof for certain operations of disjunction (and the symbol '$\sqcap$' and variants thereof for certain operations of conjunction).

[11] Fine does not use the label 'fact' for these sets, but it will prove convenient to do so.

fusion operation on *states*. Where $\mathfrak{F}$ is a state frame or a generalized state frame with fusion operation $\prod$, let me use $\prod_{\mathfrak{F}}$ for the corresponding fusion operation on $\mathfrak{F}$'s sets of states (when no confusion threatens, I will feel free to omit the subscript). For any sets of states $S_1$ and $S_2$ of the frame, $\prod_{\mathfrak{F}} \{S_1, S_2\}$ is the set of all $s_1 s_2$ with $s_1 \in S_1$ and $s_2 \in S_2$. We may generalize this idea to any set of sets of states by appealing to choice functions. Where S is a non-empty set of sets, a *choice function* on S is any function $f$ that takes each $s \in S$ into an element of s. A *selection* from a non-empty set of sets S is the image of some choice function on S – that is, a set T is a selection from S iff T = $\{f(s) : s \in S\}$ for some choice function $f$ on S. (Note that in case S contains $\varnothing$, there is no choice function on S, and therefore no selection from S either.) The formal definition of $\prod_{\mathfrak{F}}$ goes as follows:

- For $\mathcal{S}$ a non-empty set of sets of states, $\prod_{\mathfrak{F}} \mathcal{S}$ =df $\{\prod T : T$ a selection from $\mathcal{S}\}$;
- $\prod_{\mathfrak{F}} \varnothing$ =df $\{\prod \varnothing\}$.

An alternative but equivalent way of defining $\prod_{\mathfrak{F}}$ in the non-degenerate cases, which some may find more perspicuous, defines it as operating on indexed families of sets of states rather than on sets of sets of states, as follows:

- For any non-empty family $(S_i)_{i \in I}$ of sets of states, $\prod_{\mathfrak{F}} (S_i)_{i \in I}$ =df $\{\prod (s_i)_{i \in I} : (s_i)_{i \in I}$ is a family of states such that $s_i \in S_i$ for all $i \in I\}$.

One can verify that if $\mathcal{S}$ is a non-empty set of *facts*, then $\prod_{\mathfrak{F}} \mathcal{S}$ is itself a fact (and that if $(S_i)_{i \in I}$ is a non-empty family of *facts*, then $\prod_{\mathfrak{F}} (S_i)_{i \in I}$ is itself a fact).

Given any generalized state frame $\mathfrak{F}$ with underlying verification space $\mathcal{V}$, four ground-theoretic relations are defined, the first two between sets of members of $\mathcal{V}$ and members of $\mathcal{V}$, and the other ones between members of $\mathcal{V}$ and members of $\mathcal{V}$ (here I use $\prod$ instead of $\prod_{\mathfrak{F}}$):

- $\mathcal{F} \leqslant_{\mathfrak{F}} F$ (read: $\mathcal{F}$ is a *weak full ground* for $F$ in $\mathfrak{F}$) iff$_{df}$ $\prod \mathcal{F} \subseteq F$;
- $G \preccurlyeq_{\mathfrak{F}} F$ (read: $G$ is a *weak partial ground* for $F$ in $\mathfrak{F}$) iff$_{df}$ for some $\mathcal{F} \subseteq \mathcal{V}$ such that $G \in \mathcal{F}$, $\mathcal{F} \leqslant_{\mathfrak{F}} F$;
- $\mathcal{F} <_{\mathfrak{F}} F$ (read: $\mathcal{F}$ is a *strict full ground* for $F$ in $\mathfrak{F}$) iff$_{df}$ $\mathcal{F} \leqslant_{\mathfrak{F}} F$ and for no $G \in \mathcal{F}$ does $F \preccurlyeq_{\mathfrak{F}} G$;
- $G \prec_{\mathfrak{F}} F$ (read: $G$ is a *strict partial ground* for $F$ in $\mathfrak{F}$) iff$_{df}$ $G \preccurlyeq_{\mathfrak{F}} F$ but not $F \preccurlyeq_{\mathfrak{F}} G$.

Let $\mathfrak{M}$ be a generalized state model with underlying generalized state frame $\mathfrak{F}$ and verification valuation [ ]. Let [Δ] be $\{[\phi] : \phi \in \Delta\}$. The relations just defined allow one to define a notion of 'holding in $\mathfrak{M}$' for each type of sequent of the language in the obvious way:

- $\Delta \leqslant \phi$ holds in $\mathfrak{M}$ iff $[\Delta] \leqslant_{\mathfrak{F}} [\phi]$
- $\phi \preccurlyeq \psi$ holds in $\mathfrak{M}$ iff $[\phi] \preccurlyeq_{\mathfrak{F}} [\psi]$
- $\Delta < \phi$ holds in $\mathfrak{M}$ iff $[\Delta] <_{\mathfrak{F}} [\phi]$
- $\phi < \psi$ holds in $\mathfrak{M}$ iff $[\phi] <_{\mathfrak{F}} [\psi]$

A sequent $\sigma$ is then said to be a *PLG-consequence* of a set of sequents $\Sigma$ iff there is no generalized state model in which all the members of $\Sigma$ hold and $\sigma$ fails to hold. Fine's (2012b) main result is that consequence so defined and derivability in PLG coincide:

**Theorem 1** (Soundness and completeness for PLG). *A sequent $\sigma$ is derivable from a set of sequents $\Sigma$ in PLG iff $\sigma$ is a PLG-consequence of $\Sigma$.*

In the same paper, Fine also examines systems formulated in languages poorer than the language of PLG, that is, in languages which comprise less than the four types of sequents defined above. Of particular interest are two systems involving only one type of sequent, a system PLWFG for the pure logic of weak full grounding and a system PLSFG for the pure logic of strict full grounding. They are presented in the same format as PLG but with their own sets of rules – see Figures 2 and 3.

$$\frac{\Delta_1 \leqslant \phi_1 \quad \Delta_2 \leqslant \phi_2 \quad \ldots \quad \phi_1, \phi_2, \ldots \leqslant \phi}{\Delta_1, \Delta_2, \ldots \leqslant \phi} \qquad \text{Cut } (\leqslant)$$

$$\frac{}{\phi \leqslant \phi} \qquad \text{Identity}$$

**Figure 2** Rules for PLWFG

$$\frac{\Delta_1 < \phi_1 \quad \Delta_2 < \phi_2 \quad \ldots \quad \phi_1, \phi_2, \ldots, \Gamma < \psi}{\Delta_1, \Delta_2, \ldots, \Gamma < \psi} \qquad \text{Cut } (<)$$

$$\frac{\Delta, \phi < \phi}{\bot} \qquad \text{Non-Circularity } (<)$$

$$\frac{\Delta_1 < \phi \quad \Delta_2 < \phi \quad \ldots}{\Delta_1, \Delta_2, \ldots < \phi} \qquad \text{Amalgamation } (<)$$

**Figure 3** Rules for PLSFG

Fine establishes that both PLWFG and PLSFG are fragments of PLG (or, to use another standard terminology, that PLG is a conservative extension of both PLWFG and PLSFG), in the following sense:

**Theorem 2.**

1. *Let $\sigma$ be a sequent from the language of PLWFL and $\Sigma$ a set of sequents from the same language. Then $\sigma$ is derivable from $\Sigma$ in PLWFG iff $\sigma$ is derivable from $\Sigma$ in PLG.*
2. *Let $\sigma$ be a sequent from the language of PLSFL and $\Sigma$ a set of sequents from the same language. Then $\sigma$ is derivable from $\Sigma$ in PLSFG iff $\sigma$ is derivable from $\Sigma$ in PLG.*

The semantics for PLG can of course be used almost as it is to interpret the language of PLWFG and that of PLSFG: one simply has to remove the semantic clauses for the sequents that are not in the relevant language. We thus have a notion of PLWFG-consequence and one of PLWFG-consequence, and the previous theorem together with the soundness and completeness theorem for PLG allows one to establish without effort the following:

**Theorem 3** (Soundness and completeness for PLWFG and PLSFG).

1. *A sequent $\sigma$ is derivable from a set of sequents $\Sigma$ in PLWFG iff $\sigma$ is a PLWFG-consequence of $\Sigma$.*
2. *A sequent $\sigma$ is derivable from a set of sequents $\Sigma$ in PLSFG iff $\sigma$ is a PLSFG-consequence of $\Sigma$.*

Fine's approach to the pure logic of grounding has been criticized in a number of ways. Some criticisms question the properties that PLG attributes to strict full grounding. The three rules for PLSFG, or consequences thereof, have indeed been subject to objections: it has been argued that strict full grounding is not irreflexive (see Correia 2014 and Woods 2018),[12] from which it follows that Non-Circularity (<) fails; it has been argued that partial strict ground (the relation defined on page 8 and symbolized by <*, not the relation symbolized by <) is not transitive (see Schaffer 2012), from which it follows that Cut (<) fails; and the validity of Amalgamation (<) has been questioned (see deRosset 2015,

---

[12] In Correia (2014), I focus on *logical* grounding, but on the assumption that logical grounding implies metaphysical grounding, failures of irreflexivity for strict full logical grounding imply failures of irreflexivity for strict full metaphysical grounding.

Litland 2018a and Litland 2018b). These objections are important and would therefore deserve extensive discussion, but for lack of space I will leave them aside.[13]

Let me elaborate a bit on a further objection to Fine's approach, which will give me the opportunity to emphasize an important aspect of Fine's truthmaker framework. Fine's pure logic of grounding features the notion of weak full grounding. Moreover, as I announced at the beginning of this section, Fine's logic reflects the view that weak full grounding is *the basic grounding relation* in terms of which the other three grounding relations are defined, in the manner I mentioned there. This last point is absolutely clear from the semantics. But what is weak full grounding? deRosset (2013a, 2014) has argued that what Fine (2012a, 2012b) says by way of clarifying the notion is insufficient or even problematic.

I agree with deRosset on some of the objections he makes, but for the sake of the line of argumentation I am pursuing here let me just mention one particular objection which I take to be ineffective. One suggestion for making sense of weak full grounding is to take the proposed truthmaker semantics seriously, that is, as providing genuine truth-conditions for ground-theoretic claims in addition to providing a mathematically handy way of characterizing links of logical consequence between such claims. Taking the semantics seriously means holding that for any interpreted language of the sort under consideration here, there is a privileged generalized state model $\mathfrak{M}$ (an 'intended model') such that a sequent of the language – in particular, a sequent with $\leqslant$ as ground-theoretic operator – is true *tout court* iff it is true relative to $\mathfrak{M}$. deRosset denies that this suggestion allows one to correctly interpret $\leqslant$. His argument goes essentially as follows:

> Let $\psi$ be a sentence expressing that Maria is sad and $\phi$ a sentence expressing that Maria is sad or Sam is happy, and suppose that Maria is sad and Sam is not happy. Let then $\mathfrak{M}$ be a privileged model for a language comprising the sequent $\phi \leqslant \psi$. Relative to $\mathfrak{M}$, $\psi$ and $\phi$ have exactly the same exact verifiers, and therefore $\phi \leqslant \psi$ comes out as true. But $\phi \leqslant \psi$ is *not* true.

---

[13] Yet see the end of Section 2.5 for an objection against Amalgamation (<) based on the conception of grounding explored in Litland (2018b). Another objection that would deserve some discussion concerns the presence of a privileged set of facts (the verification space) in the models used by Fine: what does it mean to say that some facts but not others are 'capable' of being the semantic value of a statement? Importantly, as Fine himself (2012b) points out, given the way completeness is proved it is clear that completeness still holds if we assume that the verification space is in each model the set of all the facts. The introduction of verification spaces is accordingly not even motivated by the desire to establish completeness, contrary to what one might have thought. I point to a possible motivation in footnote 39.

As the reader may already know or will grant after reading Section 3, there are various ways in which one may justify the claim that $\phi \leqslant \psi$ is not true. Let us just take the claim for granted. What is wrong in deRosset's argument is the claim that relative to the intended model $\mathfrak{M}$, $\phi$ and $\psi$ have exactly the same exact verifiers. On Fine's approach, the verifiers of a sentence are states; states may or may not obtain; and a sentence is true just in case at least one of its verifiers obtains. This distinction between obtaining and non-obtaining (or 'actual' and 'non-actual') states and the connection between truth and obtainment are absent from Fine 2012a and Fine 2012b, but are made explicit in later work on the truthmaker framework (e.g., in Fine 2017a). Now relative to $\mathfrak{M}$, $\phi$ and $\psi$ have the same *obtaining* exact verifiers, but their exact verifiers *tout court* are distinct: for instance, the (non-obtaining) state of Sam's being happy is an exact verifier for $\phi$ but not for $\psi$. Hence, by the semantics' own lights, $\phi \leqslant \psi$ is false – as desired.

## 2.2 deRosset's 'On Weak Ground'

As I have just emphasized, deRosset is dissatisfied with Fine's treatment of the pure logic of grounding because it invokes the notion of weak full grounding, a notion which he finds obscure. In deRosset (2014), he presents a logic which features only a notion of strict full grounding (<) (deRosset has plausibly in mind the canonical notion) and the companion notion of partial strict grounding (<*).[14] His system for the 'logic of strict grounding' (LSG), as he calls it, is defined by the rules listed in Figure 4.

By the definition of <* in terms of < given on page 8, Subsumption (</<*) directly follows, Transitivity (<*) follows from Cut (<), and Non-Circularity (<*) follows from Non-Circularity (<). Non-Circularity (<), Cut (<) and Amalgamation (<) define Fine's system PLSFG which, as we saw, is a fragment of his PLG. Since Non-Circularity (<) follows from Non-Circularity (<*) and Subsumption (</<*), PLSFG is also a fragment of LSG.

On the semantic side, deRosset follows Fine: he invokes generalized state models, interprets the sequents of the language of LSG using these models, and define consequence for this language – LSG-consequence – in the same way as described above. He interprets sequents of type $\Delta < \phi$ in the same way as Fine does, and sequents of type $\phi <^* \psi$ *in the way Fine interprets sequents of type* $\phi < \psi$. (This is important to emphasize since, once again, <* and < express distinct notions.) deRosset then establishes that LSG is sound and complete relative to the proposed semantics:

---

[14] deRosset uses < instead of <* for partial strict grounding, which generates a clear risk of confusion. I stick to the Finean notation for the latter notion.

| | |
|---|---|
| $\dfrac{\Delta, \phi < \psi}{\phi <^* \psi}$ | Subsumption ($</<^*$) |
| $\dfrac{\phi <^* \psi \quad \psi <^* \chi}{\phi <^* \chi}$ | Transitivity ($<^*$) |
| $\dfrac{\phi <^* \phi}{\bot}$ | Non-Circularity ($<^*$) |
| $\dfrac{\Delta_1 < \phi_1 \quad \Delta_2 < \phi_2 \quad \ldots \quad \phi_1, \phi_2, \ldots, \Gamma < \psi}{\Delta_1, \Delta_2, \ldots, \Gamma < \psi}$ | Cut ($<$) |
| $\dfrac{\Delta_1 < \phi \quad \Delta_2 < \phi \quad \ldots}{\Delta_1, \Delta_2, \ldots < \phi}$ | Amalgamation ($<$) |

**Figure 4** Rules for LSG

**Theorem 4** (Soundness and completeness for LSG). *A sequent $\sigma$ is derivable from a set of sequents $\Sigma$ in LSG iff $\sigma$ is an LSG-consequence of $\Sigma$.*

The way he proceeds, in effect, is as follows.[15] Let LSG⁻ be the system defined exactly like LSG except that every occurrence of a sequent of type $\phi <^* \psi$ is replaced by the sequent $\phi < \psi$, and define LSG⁻-consequence simply as PLG-consequence on the language of LSG⁻. deRosset establishes that LSG⁻ is a fragment of PLG:

**Theorem 5.** *Let $\sigma$ be a sequent from the language of LSG⁻ and $\Sigma$ a set of sequents from the same language. Then $\sigma$ is derivable from $\Sigma$ in LSG⁻ iff $\sigma$ is derivable from $\Sigma$ in PLG.*

Given the definition of LSG⁻-consequence, it immediately follows that LSG⁻ is sound and complete relative to the proposed semantics for LSG⁻:

**Theorem 6** (Soundness and completeness for LSG⁻). *A sequent $\sigma$ is derivable from a set of sequents $\Sigma$ in LSG⁻ iff $\sigma$ is an LSG⁻-consequence of $\Sigma$.*

Now the difference between LSG and LSG⁻ is merely notational – the only difference is that LSG has the symbol $<^*$ where LSG⁻ has the symbol $<$.

---

[15] The way deRosset proceeds is a bit more direct, because (as I highlighted in the previous footnote) he uses the symbol $<$ instead of $<^*$ for the characterization of LSG.

Therefore, from the soundness and completeness result for LSG⁻ one can infer the soundness and completeness result for LSG.

Theorem 4 certainly has some value from a formal point of view – soundness + completeness results, in general, are indeed formally valuable. But it is not philosophically satisfactory, at least when evaluated against deRosset's initial motivation for introducing LSG – namely, to put it briefly, to get rid of weak grounding. Given its intended interpretation, the proof system is all about the familiar notion of strict full grounding and partial strict grounding, weak grounding is completely out of the picture. So far so good. But semantically, weak full grounding still plays the central role: the truth-clauses for $<$ are the same as in the semantics for PLG, the truth-clauses for $<^*$ are those for $<$ in the semantics for PLG, and the latter are ultimately formulated in terms of the semantic embodiment of weak full grounding. In a later paper (deRosset 2015), however, he proposes an alternative semantics where weak full grounding plays no role at all. This is the topic of the next section.

## 2.3 deRosset's 'Better Semantics for the Pure Logic of Ground'

deRosset (2015) cashes out the intuitive content of his alternative semantics in terms of the notion of *immediate* (or *unmediated*, as he sometimes puts it) grounding. He defines a corresponding notion of mediate grounding in terms of chains of immediate links, and he identifies the canonical notion of grounding with that mediate notion (following, in effect, Fine 2012a – see the end of Section 1.2). The semantics he proposes is then 'homophonic': a sequent of type $\Delta < \phi$ is taken to hold just in case the facts expressed by the members of $\Delta$ ground, in the canonical sense, the fact expressed by $\phi$ (and likewise for sequents of type $\phi <^* \psi$).

Let me go through the semantics in a more precise way. The basic structures invoked by deRosset are so-called *hypergraphs*.[16] Each hypergraph generates a set of labelled trees (modulo replacement of nodes by other nodes), and each such labelled tree is taken to represent a link of strict full grounding. I here follow the spirit but not the letter of deRosset's semantics: I directly start off with labelled trees (the detour via hypergraphs strikes me as unnecessary).

The labelled trees that are invoked are those defined in the Appendix (the various tree-theoretic notions that I use below are all defined there). For present purposes, I call them *grounding trees* and I call the labels of a grounding tree its *facts*. Let me adopt the following definitions:

---

[16] Litland (2015, 2018a) also models grounding using hypergraphs. I will briefly discuss Litland (2018a) in Section 2.4.

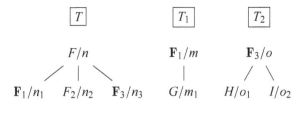

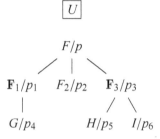

**Figure 5** Extension of a tree

- Let $T$ be a grounding tree and $(T_i)_{i \in I}$ a family of grounding trees. $T$ can be *extended with* $(T_i)_{i \in I}$ iff$_{df}$ there is a non-empty family $(l_i)_{i \in I}$ of leaves of $T$ such that for each $i \in I$, $l_i$ is occupied by the same fact as $T_i$'s root.
- Let $T$ be a grounding tree and $(T_i)_{i \in I}$ a family of grounding trees such that the former can be extended with the latter. A grounding tree $U$ *extends* $T$ *with* $(T_i)_{i \in I}$ iff$_{df}$ there is an initial subtree $U^*$ of $U$ and an isomorphism $f$ from $T$ to $U^*$ such that for any $i \in I$, the final subtree of $U$ whose root is $f(l_i)$ is isomorphic to $T_i$.

In Figure 5, $U$ extends $T$ with $T_1$ and $T_2$ (the notation $X/x$ indicates that fact $X$ occupies node $x$).

A *grounding frame* is defined as a set $\mathfrak{T}$ of grounding trees that satisfy the following closure condition:

> For any tree $T$ and family of trees $(T_i)_{i \in I}$ in $\mathfrak{T}$ such that the former can be extended with the latter, there is a grounding tree in $\mathfrak{T}$ that does extend $T$ with $(T_i)_{i \in I}$.

As the reader may anticipate, this condition will guarantee that Cut ($<$) is validated. Two further conditions on grounding frames, that of being acyclic and that of being additive, play a central role in the semantics, where these conditions are defined as follows:

- A grounding frame is *acyclic* iff$_{df}$ none of its grounding trees has a fact that appears twice on one of its branches.

- A grounding frame is *additive* iff$_{df}$ for every fact $F$ and family of non-empty sets of facts $(\mathcal{F}_i)_{i \in I}$ such that for each $i \in I$, the frame contains a grounding tree with top $F$ and bottom $\mathcal{F}_i$, the frame also contains a grounding tree with top $F$ and bottom $\bigcup_{i \in I} \mathcal{F}_i$.

As the reader has certainly anticipated, imposing the first condition will secure Non-Circularity ($<$), and imposing the second condition will secure Amalgamation ($<$).

Where $\mathfrak{T}$ is a grounding frame, define the relation $<_{\mathfrak{T}}$ between sets of facts in $\mathfrak{T}$ (where a fact in $\mathfrak{T}$ is a fact of some grounding tree in $\mathfrak{T}$) and facts in $\mathfrak{T}$, and the binary relation $<^{*}_{\mathfrak{T}}$ between facts in $\mathfrak{T}$, as follows:

- $\mathcal{F} <_{\mathfrak{T}} F$ iff$_{df}$ there is a grounding tree $T$ in $\mathfrak{T}$ such that (i) $F = T$'s top and (ii) $\mathcal{F} = T$'s bottom;
- $G <^{*}_{\mathfrak{T}} F$ iff$_{df}$ for some set of facts $\mathcal{F}$ in $\mathfrak{T}$ such that $G \in \mathcal{F}$, $\mathcal{F} <_{\mathfrak{T}} F$.

The language deRosset focuses on is the same as in his 2014 paper: the sequents are those constructed with $<$ and $<^{*}$.[17] A *grounding model* for that language is a pair $\langle \mathfrak{T}, [\,] \rangle$, where $\mathfrak{T}$ is a grounding frame and $[\,]$ (interpretation) is a function taking each basic sentence of the language into a fact of some tree in $\mathfrak{T}$. A grounding model is said to be *acyclic / additive* iff the underlying grounding frame is acyclic / additive. The notion of holding in a grounding model $\mathfrak{M}$ with underlying grounding frame $\mathfrak{T}$ and interpretation function $[\,]$ is then naturally defined as follows:

- $\Delta < \phi$ holds in $\mathfrak{M}$ iff $[\Delta] <_{\mathfrak{T}} [\phi]$
- $\psi <^{*} \phi$ holds in $\mathfrak{M}$ iff $[\psi] <^{*}_{\mathfrak{T}} [\phi]$

deRosset characterizes four systems using this semantics. One of them is LSG as previously axiomatized (see page 17). The other three are subsystems of LSG, obtained by removing rules from its charaterization: B (the 'base logic') is the system defined by Cut ($<$), Subsumption ($</<^{*}$) and Transitivity ($<^{*}$) only, system BNC is defined by adding Non-Circularity ($<^{*}$) and system BA by adding Amalgamation ($<$) instead. Without much surprise, the characterization results he establishes are as follows:

**Theorem 7** (Soundness and completeness for LSG and its subsystems). *Let $\sigma$ be a sequent and $\Sigma$ a set of sequents of the language. Then:*

---

[17] As in the 2014 paper, he uses $<$ instead of $<^{*}$. But here, unlike in the 2014 paper, he explicitly attributes to Fine the view that the symbol $<$ in his system PLG expresses partial strict grounding. This is of course incorrect: once again, in Fine's notation $<$ expresses strict partial grounding, and it is $<^{*}$ that expresses partial strict grounding.

1. $\sigma$ is derivable from $\Sigma$ in B iff $\sigma$ holds in every grounding model *in which all the members of* $\Sigma$ *hold*.
2. $\sigma$ is derivable from $\Sigma$ in BNC iff $\sigma$ holds in every acyclic grounding model *in which all the members of* $\Sigma$ *hold*.
3. $\sigma$ is derivable from $\Sigma$ in BA iff $\sigma$ holds in every additive grounding model *in which all the members of* $\Sigma$ *hold*.
4. $\sigma$ is derivable from $\Sigma$ in LSG iff $\sigma$ holds in every acyclic and additive grounding model *in which all the members of* $\Sigma$ *hold*.

As I emphasized at the outset, deRosset advertises his semantics as being based on the idea that every link of grounding in the canonical sense can be seen as the result of chaining links of *immediate* grounding. Let me close this section with two remarks about this gloss on the semantics.

My first remark is that the gloss is not formally implemented in the semantics. deRosset thinks of a grounding tree of height 2 (i.e., whose nodes are, apart from its root, only children of the root) as representing the fact occupying the root as being immediately grounded in the facts whose set occupies the set of the tree's leaves. But nothing forces this interpretation of the grounding trees: as far as the characterization results are concerned, the grounding trees of height 2 may just as well be interpreted as representing the fact occupying the root as being grounded *in the canonical sense* in the facts whose set occupies the set of the tree's leaves.

The second remark is that this very fact about the interpretation of the semantics, far from being a problem, may actually be argued to be a positive feature of the semantics: as I have argued elsewhere (Correia 2021a: 5968), the view that there are facts that are grounded in the canonical sense without being immediately grounded cannot be lightly discarded.

## 2.4 Litland on Bicollective Grounding

As I emphasized in Section 1.2, Litland takes seriously the idea that there can be cases where several facts are metaphysically strictly fully grounded in some facts without the grounded facts being individually grounded in (some of) the grounding facts. To use Litland's (2018a) terminology, the idea is that metaphysical strict full grounding is *bicollective* rather than, as orthodoxy has it, (merely) left-collective.[18] Litland (2016, 2018a) proposes two very different

---

[18] The view Litland explores is one according to which both the ground and the groundee can be empty, singular or (irreducibly) plural. Expanding the terminology I introduced in Section 1.1, it is a view according to which metaphysical strict full grounding may be dubbed '(zero or one or many)-to-(zero or one or many)'.

semantics for the logic of bicollective grounding. The first one is a truthmaker semantics, the second one a graph-theoretic semantics.

### 2.4.1 Litland (2016)

The semantics in Litland (2016) is very much like Fine's semantics for PLG.[19] The object language Litland focuses on is like the language of Fine's PLG but with a few differences: it has, in addition to the four Finean ground-theoretic operators $<, \leqslant, \preccurlyeq$ and $\prec$, the extra operator $\npreccurlyeq$; and the sequents of the language all take a set of basic sentences on the left *and on the right*, with no cardinality restrictions on these sets. $\Delta \npreccurlyeq \Gamma$ is intended to express the negation of $\Delta \preccurlyeq \Gamma$.

Litland, like Fine, uses generalized state models to interpret his sequents. Relative to every generalized state frame $\mathfrak{F}$ with underlying verification space $\mathcal{V}$, five ground-theoretic relations between sets of facts and sets of facts are defined (here again I use $\sqcap$ for $\sqcap_{\mathfrak{F}}$):

- $\mathcal{F} \leqslant_{\mathfrak{F}} \mathcal{G}$ iff$_{df}$ $\sqcap \mathcal{F} \subseteq \sqcap \mathcal{G}$;
- $\mathcal{F} \preccurlyeq_{\mathfrak{F}} \mathcal{G}$ iff$_{df}$ for some $\mathcal{F}^* \subseteq \mathcal{V}$ such that $\mathcal{F} \subseteq \mathcal{F}^*$, $\mathcal{F}^* \leqslant_{\mathfrak{F}} \mathcal{G}$;[20]
- $\mathcal{F} \npreccurlyeq_{\mathfrak{F}} \mathcal{G}$ iff$_{df}$ it is not the case that $\mathcal{F} \preccurlyeq_{\mathfrak{F}} \mathcal{G}$;
- $\mathcal{F} <_{\mathfrak{F}} \mathcal{G}$ iff$_{df}$ $\mathcal{F} \leqslant_{\mathfrak{F}} \mathcal{G}$ and $\mathcal{G} \npreccurlyeq_{\mathfrak{F}} \mathcal{F}$;
- $\mathcal{F} \prec_{\mathfrak{F}} \mathcal{G}$ iff$_{df}$ $\mathcal{F} \preccurlyeq_{\mathfrak{F}} \mathcal{G}$ and $\mathcal{G} \npreccurlyeq_{\mathfrak{F}} \mathcal{F}$.

Without surprise, the notion of holding in a generalized state model $\mathfrak{M}$ is defined as follows, where $\mathfrak{F}$ is $\mathfrak{M}$'s underlying generalized state frame and [ ] is $\mathfrak{M}$'s valuation function:

- $\Delta \leqslant \Gamma$ holds in $\mathfrak{M}$ iff $[\Delta] \leqslant_{\mathfrak{F}} [\Gamma]$
- $\Delta \preccurlyeq \Gamma$ holds in $\mathfrak{M}$ iff $[\Delta] \preccurlyeq_{\mathfrak{F}} [\Gamma]$
- $\Delta \npreccurlyeq \Gamma$ holds in $\mathfrak{M}$ iff $[\Delta] \npreccurlyeq_{\mathfrak{F}} [\Gamma]$
- $\Delta < \Gamma$ holds in $\mathfrak{M}$ iff $[\Delta] <_{\mathfrak{F}} [\Gamma]$
- $\Delta \prec \Gamma$ holds in $\mathfrak{M}$ iff $[\Delta] \prec_{\mathfrak{F}} [\Gamma]$

Consequence is defined as before.

Even though Litland's semantics is a truthmaker semantics of roughly the same sort as Fine's semantics for PLG, it cannot be said to be strictly speaking an *extension* of it. The semantics for the sequents of type $\Delta \leqslant \phi$ in Fine's logic

---

[19] I am referring to the semantics introduced in §3 of Litland (2016). In §6, Litland enriches the language with special basic sentences and modifies the semantics accordingly in order to establish soundness and completeness for his own system and for a variant of Fine's PLG. The main points I highlight below can also be made if the modified semantics is assumed instead.

[20] Litland's *definiens* is actually 'for some fact $F \in \mathcal{V}$, $\mathcal{F} \cup \{F\} \leqslant_{\mathfrak{F}} \mathcal{G}$', but since Litland assumes that verification spaces are closed under $\sqcap$ (he does this in order to simplify the logic), the two *definientia* are equivalent.

is the same as the semantics for the sequents of type $\Delta \leqslant \{\phi\}$ in Litland's logic, and therefore the two logics fully agree regarding the behaviour of the restriction of weak full grounding to cases involving individual groundees. But things are different when it comes to strict full grounding. For instance, as Litland notes, Amalgamation (<) as formulated in the language of the bicollective logic, namely:

$$\frac{\Delta_1 < \{\phi\} \quad \Delta_2 < \{\phi\} \quad \ldots}{\Delta_1, \Delta_2, \ldots < \{\phi\}}$$

is not validated by his semantics. This fact need not be seen as a problem – as I have stressed in Section 2.1, Litland (2018a) himself explicitly argues against Amalgamation (<). But let me mention two consequences of the semantics that look more problematic. Both are discussed by Litland (2016).

The first consequence is that the following rule is validated (I take the label from Litland 2018a):

$$\frac{\Delta < \Gamma}{\Delta < \Gamma, \Delta} \qquad \text{Self-Ground}$$

Granted that < expresses an explanatory relation, this does not sound acceptable. In the 2016 paper, Litland plays down the problem (page 548), but in Litland (2018a) he takes it seriously (page 147). A natural way out, which he does not himself consider in that paper, is to adopt the following definition of $<_{\mathfrak{F}}$ instead of the original one[21]:

- $\mathcal{F} <_{\mathfrak{F}} \mathcal{G}$ iff$_{df}$ $\mathcal{F} \leqslant_{\mathfrak{F}} \mathcal{G}$ and for all $\mathcal{G}^* \subseteq \mathcal{G}$ with $\mathcal{G}^* \neq \varnothing$, $\mathcal{G}^* \not\leqslant_{\mathfrak{F}} \mathcal{F}$.

On this account, $\Delta < \Gamma, \Delta$ fails to hold in any model provided that $\Delta \neq \varnothing$.

The second consequence concerns the question of what grounds conjunctive facts, a question we will discuss in some detail in Section 3. As we will see, the standard treatment of conjunctions in truthmaker semantics has it that a conjunction is exactly verified by a state $s$ iff $s$ is the fusion of two states $s_1$ and $s_2$ such that $s_1$ exactly verifies one of the conjuncts and $s_2$ exactly verifies the other conjunct. Given this treatment of conjunctions, all sequents of type $\phi \wedge \psi \leqslant \phi, \psi$ hold in every model, and therefore no sequent of type $\phi, \psi < \phi \wedge \psi$ can hold in a model. Litland admits that this is a problem if we think of strict full grounding as being explanatory. Since $\Delta < \Gamma$ holds in a model under my alternative definition of $<_{\mathfrak{F}}$ only if $\Delta < \Gamma$ holds in that model under Litland's definition, my alternative definition does nothing to solve the problem.

---

[21] Thanks to Litland for suggesting in personal communication this formulation of the definition, which is a bit simpler than another, equivalent formulation that I initially came up with.

### 2.4.2 Litland (2018a)

As previously announced, Litland (2018a) offers another, graph-theoretic semantics for bicollective grounding. In fact, he also puts forward a graph-theoretic semantics for the Finean notions of grounding, which is essentially the same semantics as deRosset's (2015) when restricted to the notions deRosset aims to characterize.[22] It would take me too far to give the reader a faithful summary of the account, so let me just get to the bare bones.

Just like deRosset's (2015) semantics, Litland's semantics can be reformulated directly in terms of labelled trees, without appealing to hypergraphs. The basic idea is to define a grounding tree, not as a labelled tree *tout court*, but as a labelled tree whose labels are *sets*. In contrast with the semantics presented in Section 2.3, we take the facts of a grounding tree to be the members of its labels rather than the labels themselves. As before, we then define grounding frames as sets of grounding trees satisfying certain properties (meant to guarantee that bicollective notions of grounding satisfy desired conditions, e.g., transitivity / cut conditions), and grounding models as grounding frames equipped with an interpretation function. The definition of bicollective strict full grounding relative to a grounding frame $\mathfrak{T}$ is then taken to go as follows:

- $\mathcal{F} <_\mathfrak{T} \mathcal{G}$ iff$_{df}$ there is a grounding tree $T$ in $\mathfrak{T}$ such that (i) $\mathcal{G} = T$'s top and (ii) $\mathcal{F} =$ the union of $T$'s bottom.

(Compare with the definition of $<_\mathfrak{T}$ on page 20, especially the second clause.)

It is clear that even after suitable conditions on grounding frames have been imposed to ensure that bicollective $<$ satisfies desired principles of cut and irreflexivity, Self-Ground will not be validated. It also seems clear that the proposed semantics is not inhospitable to the view that sequents of type $\phi, \psi < \phi \wedge \psi$ can hold.

## 2.5 Litland's 'Grounding Ground' and 'Pure Logic of Iterated Full Ground'

In his 2017 and 2018b papers, Litland develops in proof-theoretic fashion a logic of (merely left-collective) strict full grounding. The logic is based on an account of strict full grounding which in turn is based on two assumptions: (a) there is a distinction between arguments that are metaphysically explanatory (arguments whose premises provide metaphysical explanations of why their

---

[22] The approach is also developed in Litland (2015) for non-bicollective notions, but in a different form. Litland (2018a) advertises his presentation of the approach as correcting 'minor infelicities' in both deRosset (2015) and Litland (2015).

conclusions hold) and arguments that are not, and (b) there is a distinction between factive (<) and non-factive ($\Rightarrow$) strict full grounding. The core of the account features the following two biconditionals:

(i) $\Delta \Rightarrow \phi$ holds iff there is an explanatory argument from (exactly) $\Delta$ to $\phi$;
(ii) $\Delta < \phi$ holds iff $\Delta \Rightarrow \phi$ and all the members of $\Delta$ hold.

(ii) records an obvious connection between factive and non-factive strict full grounding which is standardly acknowledged. (i) is Litland's own contribution.

Litland (2017) offers an introduction rule and an elimination rule for both $\Rightarrow$ and <. Litland (2018b) keeps the same rules but add two elimination rules, one for each operator, in order to guarantee that the system conforms to the view that the introduction rule(s) for an operator *define* that operator – a view that Litland adopts but which is not forced upon those who are sympathetic to (i) and (ii) above. The elimination rules present in both Litland (2017) and Litland (2018b) are called *plain*, those that are added in Litland (2018b) are called *explanatory*. I will leave the latter rules aside in what follows.

The proof-theory offered by Litland is quite complicated, especially because of the elimination rules. But the introduction rules are easy to state, and from them plus a few consequences of the plain elimination rules one can already derive interesting results.

The introduction rules are as follows:

$$\dfrac{\overline{\Delta}^{\,1}\\ \mathcal{E}\\ \phi}{\Delta \Rightarrow \phi}\,{}^1 \qquad \Rightarrow\text{-Introduction}$$

$$\dfrac{\Delta \quad \Delta \Rightarrow \phi}{\Delta < \phi} \qquad <\text{-Introduction}$$

The second introduction rule can be immediately extracted from the right-to-left direction of biconditional (ii) above. The first introduction rule can also be extracted from the right-to-left direction of the corresponding biconditional, namely (i) above, but with a little twist. Unlike the second rule, it is a rule with discharge of assumptions. It may be read: conclude $\Delta \Rightarrow \phi$ from any explanatory argument $\mathcal{E}$ with $\phi$ as conclusion where $\Delta$ are all and only the premises on which $\phi$ depends, and discharge all the premises when drawing the conclusion.

Litland takes both introduction rules to generate explanatory arguments. The view that <-Introduction generates explanatory arguments may be justified in a natural way by invoking the view that (a) for $\Delta < \phi$ to hold *just is* for the members of $\Delta$ and $\Delta \Rightarrow \phi$ to hold and the view that (b) the truth of a conjunction is explained, in the relevant sense, in the truth of its conjuncts. By contrast, it is not clear (to me, at least) how to justify the view that $\Rightarrow$-Introduction generates explanatory arguments. However, the view that it does has an important consequence:

(C1) If $\Delta \Rightarrow \phi$ has been established by an application of $\Rightarrow$-Introduction, then $\Delta \Rightarrow \phi$ is zero-grounded in the non-factive sense, that is, $\varnothing \Rightarrow (\Delta \Rightarrow \phi)$ holds.

This consequence is important for two reasons. The first one is that it tells us that certain grounding facts are themselves grounded, and it tells us what they are grounded in. The second reason is that it provides an illustration of the prima facie somewhat obscure notion of zero-grounding.

The view that <-Introduction generates explanatory arguments has the following consequence:

(C2) $(\Delta, \Delta \Rightarrow \phi) \Rightarrow (\Delta < \phi)$ holds.

Using (C2) and <-Introduction, one can infer:

(C3) If the members of $\Delta$ and $\Delta \Rightarrow \phi$ hold, then $(\Delta, \Delta \Rightarrow \phi) < (\Delta < \phi)$ holds.

We can get 'simplified' versions of (C2) and (C3) by using (C1). The plain elimination rule for $\Rightarrow$ allows one to establish the strong cut rule for $\Rightarrow$, namely:

$$\frac{\Delta_1 \Rightarrow \phi_1 \quad \Delta_2 \Rightarrow \phi_2 \quad \ldots \quad \phi_1, \phi_2, \ldots, \Gamma \Rightarrow \psi}{\Delta_1, \Delta_2, \ldots, \Gamma \Rightarrow \psi} \quad \text{Cut } (\Rightarrow)$$

Given Cut ($\Rightarrow$), (C1) and (C2) yield the following:

(C4) If $\Delta \Rightarrow \phi$ has been established by an application of $\Rightarrow$-Introduction, then $\Delta \Rightarrow (\Delta < \phi)$ holds.

Using (C4) and <-Introduction, one can then infer:

(C5) If $\Delta \Rightarrow \phi$ has been established by an application of $\Rightarrow$-Introduction, and if all the members of $\Delta$ hold, then $\Delta < (\Delta < \phi)$ holds.

This latter principle is a restricted version of the principle which states that factive strict full grounding is *superinternal*, that is, the principle that if $\Delta < \phi$ holds, then $\Delta < (\Delta < \phi)$ also holds – a principle explicitly endorsed by Bennett (2011) and deRosset (2013b).

$\Rightarrow$-Introduction and the plain elimination rule for $\Rightarrow$ together guarantee that something stronger than (C1) is the case, namely:

(C1*) If $\Delta \Rightarrow \phi$ holds, then $\varnothing \Rightarrow (\Delta \Rightarrow \phi)$ holds.

Using this, one of course obtains strengthened versions of (C4) and (C5):

(C4*) If $\Delta \Rightarrow \phi$ holds, then $\Delta \Rightarrow (\Delta < \phi)$ holds.
(C5*) If $\Delta \Rightarrow \phi$ holds, and if all the members of $\Delta$ hold, then $\Delta < (\Delta < \phi)$ holds.

Taking on board the plain elimination rule for $<$, one gets the left-to-right direction of biconditional (ii) above.[23] Using (C5*), one then gets:

(C6) If $\Delta < \phi$ holds, then $\Delta < (\Delta < \phi)$ holds.

This is the unrestricted principle of superinternality.

As we saw, the 2017 logic has Cut ($\Rightarrow$). It also has Cut ($<$). We also saw that the logic has left-factivity for $<$: if $\Delta < \phi$ holds, then all the members of $\Delta$ hold. It also has right-factivity: if $\Delta < \phi$ holds, then $\phi$ holds. Non-Circularity ($<$) is also validated by the logic, thanks to a specific non-circularity principle governing certain arguments containing explanatory arguments introduced by Litland. Interestingly, the counterpart of the principle for $\Rightarrow$ is *not* validated by the logic, and Litland in fact suggests a counterexample (see 2018b: 419). Finally, the logic validates neither Amalgamation ($<$) nor its non-factive counterpart: given that there is an explanatory argument from $\Delta$ to $\phi$ and another explanatory argument from $\Gamma$ to $\phi$, there is no guarantee that there is an explanatory argument from $\Delta, \Gamma$ to $\phi$ – whether or not the members of $\Delta, \Gamma$ hold.[24]

Let me close this section by pointing to a fact that the reader may have noticed: (C1)–(C6), (C1*), (C4*) and (C5*) all involve iterations of ground-theoretic operators. This is worth emphasizing, because all the other approaches to the pure logic of grounding that I have presented above either impose a grammatical ban on such iterations, or are silent on the principles that govern propositions that involve them.

---

[23] Likewise, the plain elimination rule for $\Rightarrow$ secures the left-to-right direction of biconditional (i), but – importantly – only in spirit, not in letter: the language of the logic does not allow one to treat as conclusions formulas which state that there is an explanatory argument from some premiss to some conclusion.

[24] As Litland (2018b) suggests (see also Correia 2014), one way of securing amalgamation is to work with distributive notions. Let $\rightarrowtail$ be $<$ or $\Rightarrow$ (or any other merely left-collective operator, for that matter). Define its distributive mate $\rightarrowtail_d$ as follows: $\Delta \rightarrowtail_d \phi$ iff for some covering $\{\Delta_i : i \in I\}$ of $\Delta$, $\Delta_i \rightarrowtail_d \phi$ holds for all $i \in I$. (A covering of a set $S$ is a set of sets whose union is identical to $S$.) Then by its mere definition, $\rightarrowtail_d$ obeys the amalgamation principle. Interestingly, if $\rightarrowtail$ obeys the non-circularity principle, so does $\rightarrowtail_d$, and likewise, if $\rightarrowtail$ obeys the strong cut principle, so does $\rightarrowtail_d$.

## 3 Impure Logics

The pure logic of grounding is of limited interest. It is of course important to be clear on the structural properties of the various grounding relations we are interested in, but we also want to know how grounding interacts with other notions, in particular with the notions expressed by the so-called logical constants. The impure logic of grounding deals with the interaction between grounding and other notions, insofar as these notions are involved in the grounds and the groundees. Thus, for instance, principles of the impure logic of grounding may include the principle that $\phi, \psi < \phi \wedge \psi$ holds whenever $\phi$ and $\psi$ both hold, or, where $\Diamond$ is a possibility operator, the principle that $\phi < \Diamond \phi$ holds whenever $\phi$ holds. The literature on the impure logic of grounding has massively focused on the interaction of grounding with conjunction, disjunction and negation. In this section, I will focus exclusively on the interaction with these three notions. Interaction with the quantifiers and with lambda abstraction will be (somewhat briefly) discussed in Section 4.2.[25]

This section is divided into seven parts. The first four parts (Sections 3.1 to 3.4) discuss logics for notions of grounding that I classify as 'worldly', the next two parts (Sections 3.5 and 3.6) logics for notions of grounding that I classify as 'representational' (I introduce the worldly / representational distinction briefly in Section 3.5, and say more in Section 4.1). The last part (Section 3.7) briefly presents works that have not been discussed in the previous parts. The decision of which works should feature in this last part as opposed to the previous parts has been guided by my intention to prioritize works which establish soundness and completeness for systems relative to associated semantics, and other works closely related to the latter.

### 3.1 Fine's 'Guide to Ground' (Semantic Side)

Fine's (2012b) semantics for the pure logic of grounding can easily be extended to a semantics for an impure logic by interpreting the standard connectives $\wedge$, $\vee$ and $\neg$ in the exact verification framework. Fine (2012a) suggests a way of doing just that.[26] The presentation of the semantics offered in the 2012a paper is somewhat informal; let me be a bit more precise, taking the semantics of

---

[25] The interaction with universal quantification is typically treated roughly like the interaction with conjunction, and likewise for existential quantification and disjunction (see Schnieder 2011; Fine 2012a; Correia 2014; Korbmacher 2018a and 2018b; deRosset and Fine 2023). On the interaction with lambda abstraction, see Fine (2012a). On the interaction with another notion that many have thought is a logical notion, viz. identity, see Shumener (2020).

[26] This interpretation of the connectives and variants thereof appear in many of his subsequent works. See Fine (2017b) for a systematic treatment.

the 2012b paper as my starting point (see Correia 2023). I previously stressed (footnote 5) that the extension of the 2012b semantics to be presented here requires a conception of the Finean grounding relations as non-factive. It will be important to keep this in mind.

The language in which the logic is formulated is like the language of the pure logic as specified in Fine (2012b), except that the basic sentences are now taken to be constructed from a pool of atomic sentences, the connectives ∧, ∨ and ¬ and a pair of brackets in the usual way. The language is interpreted in structures that are similar to, but not identical with, the ones that were used for the pure logic.

Before introducing these structures, let me define two binary operations $\sqcap_\mathfrak{F}$ and $\sqcup_\mathfrak{F}$ on sets of states relative to an arbitrary state frame (generalized or not) $\mathfrak{F}$:

- $S_1 \sqcap_\mathfrak{F} S_2 =_{df} \prod_\mathfrak{F} \{S_1, S_2\}$
- $S_1 \sqcup_\mathfrak{F} S_2 =_{df} S_1 \cup S_2 \cup (S_1 \sqcap_\mathfrak{F} S_2)$

(As with $\prod$, I will feel free to omit the indices when no confusion threatens.) Given the role $\sqcap_\mathfrak{F}$ and $\sqcup_\mathfrak{F}$ play in the semantics of ∧ and ∨ (see below), it is appropriate to view $\sqcap_\mathfrak{F}$ as an operation of conjunction on sets of states and $\sqcup_\mathfrak{F}$ as an operation of disjunction on sets of states. Given the role $\prod_\mathfrak{F}$ plays in the semantics of ∧, it is also appropriate to view $\prod_\mathfrak{F}$ as a generalized operation of conjunction on sets of states, one that can operate on an arbitrary number (including 0) of sets of states. A generalized operation of disjunction on sets of states can also be defined:

- For $S$ a non-empty set of sets of states, $\bigsqcup_\mathfrak{F} S =_{df} \prod_\mathfrak{F} S_1 \cup \prod_\mathfrak{F} S_2 \cup \ldots$, where $S_1, S_2, \ldots$ are all the non-empty subsets of $S$.

(I leave aside the question of how $\bigsqcup_\mathfrak{F} \varnothing$ should be defined.) We will need this operation at a later point.

We still call the models for the new language *generalized state models*, but they are now taken to be tuples $\langle S, \prod, \mathcal{V}, [\,]^+, [\,]^- \rangle$ where:

- $\langle S, \prod, \mathcal{V} \rangle$ is a generalized state frame that satisfies the following closure conditions:
  – for any $F_1, F_2 \in \mathcal{V}$, $F_1 \sqcap_\mathfrak{F} F_2 \in \mathcal{V}$;
  – for any $F_1, F_2 \in \mathcal{V}$, $F_1 \sqcup_\mathfrak{F} F_2 \in \mathcal{V}$;

- $[\,]^+$ (verification valuation) and $[\,]^-$ (falsification valuation) are two functions which take each atomic sentence of the language into a member of $\mathcal{V}$.

Thus, the new models differ from the original models in three ways. First, the underlying frames are not any generalized state frames: they must satisfy the specified closure conditions. The restriction is motivated by the way conjunction and disjunction are to be interpreted. Second, instead of involving one valuation function, they involve two: one that represents exact verification, and another one that represents exact *falsification*. The latter notion is new, but easy to grasp once one has grasped the notion of exact verification. The idea of having two valuation functions is motivated by the way negation is to be interpreted. The third difference is, without surprise, that these two functions map every *atom* (rather than every *basic sentence*) of the language into a member of the verification space of the associated model.

Given a generalized state model $\langle S, \sqcap, \mathcal{V}, [\,]^+, [\,]^- \rangle$, the verification relation $\Vdash$ and the falsification relation $\dashv\!\vdash$ between states and basic sentences are defined inductively as follows:

- $s \Vdash \phi$ iff $s \in [\phi]^+$
  $s \dashv\!\vdash \phi$ iff $s \in [\phi]^-$    for $\phi$ atomic
- $s \Vdash \neg\phi$ iff $s \dashv\!\vdash \phi$
  $s \dashv\!\vdash \neg\phi$ iff $s \Vdash \phi$
- $s \Vdash \phi \wedge \psi$ iff for some $s_1$ and $s_2$ such that $s = s_1 s_2$, $s_1 \Vdash \phi$ and $s_2 \Vdash \psi$
  $s \dashv\!\vdash \phi \wedge \psi$ iff $s \dashv\!\vdash \phi$ or $s \dashv\!\vdash \psi$ or $s \dashv\!\vdash \phi \vee \psi$
- $s \Vdash \phi \vee \psi$ iff $s \Vdash \phi$ or $s \Vdash \psi$ or $s \Vdash \phi \wedge \psi$
  $s \dashv\!\vdash \phi \vee \psi$ iff for some $s_1$ and $s_2$ such that $s = s_1 s_2$, $s_1 \dashv\!\vdash \phi$ and $s_2 \dashv\!\vdash \psi$

We may extend $[\,]^+$ and $[\,]^-$ to arbitrary basic formulas by putting $[\phi]^+ = \{s : s \Vdash \phi\}$ and $[\phi]^- = \{s : s \dashv\!\vdash \phi\}$. We then have:

- $[\neg\phi]^+ = [\phi]^-$
  $[\neg\phi]^- = [\phi]^+$
- $[\phi \wedge \psi]^+ = [\phi]^+ \sqcap [\psi]^+$
  $[\phi \wedge \psi]^- = [\phi]^- \sqcup [\psi]^-$
- $[\phi \vee \psi]^+ = [\phi]^+ \sqcup [\psi]^+$
  $[\phi \vee \psi]^- = [\phi]^- \sqcap [\psi]^-$

The requirement that $\mathcal{V}$ should satisfy the closure conditions mentioned in the definition of generalized state models guarantees that both $[\phi]^+$ and $[\phi]^-$ are members of $\mathcal{V}$ for any basic sentence $\phi$. Importantly, if $S_1$ and $S_2$ are *facts* of the model (i.e., sets of states closed under $\sqcap$), then not only is it the case that $S_1 \sqcap S_2$ is also a fact, but the same also holds of $S_1 \sqcup S_2$. It follows that the closure conditions are automatically satisfied if $\mathcal{V}$ is the set of all the facts of the model.[27] The notion of *holding in a model* for sequents of the language is defined exactly as it was in the pure logic.

Fine (2012a) does not investigate the principles governing the interaction between grounding and truth-functions that his semantics delivers.[28] Let me go some way in that direction, taking inspiration from Correia (2010) (which will be the focus of the next section).

The semantics validates the following interaction principles:

$$\frac{\Delta < \phi \quad \Gamma < \psi}{\Delta, \Gamma < \phi \wedge \psi} \qquad \wedge\text{-Introduction 1}$$

$$\frac{\Delta < \phi}{\Delta < \phi \vee \psi} \qquad \frac{\Delta < \psi}{\Delta < \phi \vee \psi} \qquad \vee\text{-Introduction 1}$$

$$\frac{\Delta, \phi \wedge \psi < \chi}{\Delta, \phi, \psi < \chi} \qquad \wedge\text{-Elimination}$$

$$\frac{\Delta, \phi \vee \psi < \chi}{\Delta, \phi < \chi} \qquad \frac{\Delta, \phi \vee \psi < \chi}{\Delta, \psi < \chi} \qquad \vee\text{-Elimination}$$

$$\frac{\Delta < \phi}{\Delta < \neg\neg\phi} \qquad \neg\neg\text{-Introduction}$$

$$\frac{\Delta, \neg\neg\phi < \psi}{\Delta, \phi < \psi} \qquad \neg\neg\text{-Elimination}$$

To this list, one can add the principles that result from the first four principles by replacing $\phi$ by $\neg\phi$, $\psi$ by $\neg\psi$, $\phi \wedge \psi$ by $\neg(\phi \vee \psi)$ and $\phi \vee \psi$ by $\neg(\phi \wedge \psi)$ – I will dub principles that result from such replacements *duals* of the original principles.

---

[27] An alternative but equivalent semantics can be formulated that eschews the need for falsification valuations. Take the models to be defined as above but with two modifications: (i) get rid of falsification valuations and (ii) take the verification valuations to assign elements of the verification spaces *both to atoms and negated atoms*. Then define ⊩ by means of the following clauses:

- $s \Vdash \phi$ iff $s \in [\phi]$   for $\phi$ an atomic sentence or the negation of an atomic sentence
- $s \Vdash \neg\neg\phi$ iff $s \Vdash \phi$
- $s \Vdash \phi \wedge \psi$ iff for some $s_1$ and $s_2$ such that $s = s_1 s_2$, $s_1 \Vdash \phi$ and $s_2 \Vdash \psi$
- $s \Vdash \neg(\phi \wedge \psi)$ iff $s \Vdash \neg\phi$ or $s \Vdash \neg\psi$ or $s \Vdash \neg(\phi \vee \psi)$
- $s \Vdash \phi \vee \psi$ iff $s \Vdash \phi$ or $s \Vdash \psi$ or $s \Vdash \phi \wedge \psi$
- $s \Vdash \neg(\phi \vee \psi)$ iff for some $s_1$ and $s_2$ such that $s = s_1 s_2$, $s_1 \Vdash \neg\phi$ and $s_2 \Vdash \neg\psi$

In this framework, exact falsification can be defined in the obvious way: $s$ exactly falsifies $\phi$ iff$_{\text{df}}$ $s$ exactly verifies $\neg\phi$.

[28] He discusses interaction principles of that sort, but which correspond to a quite different conception of grounding (see Section 3.5). Fine is aware of the mismatch between the interaction principles he discusses and the proposed semantics – see page 74, footnote 22.

The following introduction principles involving *weak* full grounding, as well as the duals of the first two principles, are also validated:

$$\frac{}{\phi, \psi \leqslant \phi \wedge \psi} \qquad \wedge\text{-Introduction } (\leqslant)$$

$$\frac{}{\phi \leqslant \phi \vee \psi} \qquad \frac{}{\psi \leqslant \phi \vee \psi} \qquad \vee\text{-Introduction } (\leqslant)$$

$$\frac{}{\phi \leqslant \neg\neg\phi} \qquad \neg\neg\text{-Introduction } (\leqslant)$$

Some might expect that a logic of strict full grounding should validate the same principles but with < replacing ⩽. This is true of some logics (see Section 3.5), but not of this one. It is immediate that $\phi < \neg\neg\phi$ cannot hold in a generalized state model: for any such model with underlying frame $\mathfrak{F}$ and verification valuation $[\,]^+$, $[\phi]^+ = [\neg\neg\phi]^+$ and therefore $[\neg\neg\phi]^+ \preccurlyeq_\mathfrak{F} [\phi]^+$. It is equally clear that $\phi < \phi \wedge \phi$ and $\phi < \phi \vee \phi$ cannot hold in a generalized state model: relative to any such model, $\phi$, $\phi \wedge \phi$ and $\phi \vee \phi$ have the very same verifiers. Likewise, $\neg\phi < \neg(\phi \wedge \phi)$ and $\neg\phi < \neg(\phi \vee \phi)$ cannot hold in a generalized state model.

However, restricted versions of the introduction principles that involve ∧ and ∨, as well as their duals, are validated. Let me borrow Litland's (2016) symbol ⋠, which I take here to stand for the negation of the Finean (non-bicollective) ≼. The restricted introduction principles are the following:

$$\frac{\phi \wedge \psi \not\preccurlyeq \phi \quad \phi \wedge \psi \not\preccurlyeq \psi}{\phi, \psi < \phi \wedge \psi} \qquad \wedge\text{-Introduction 2}$$

$$\frac{\phi \vee \psi \not\preccurlyeq \phi}{\phi < \phi \vee \psi} \qquad \frac{\phi \vee \psi \not\preccurlyeq \psi}{\psi < \phi \vee \psi} \qquad \vee\text{-Introduction 2}$$

Equivalent principles can be formulated using < rather than ⋠, but these principles are more perspicuous.[29]

Let me close this section with the question of how to modify the semantics in order to get a proper semantic characterization of *factive* notions of grounding. The question is easily answered (see Correia 2023, section 2). Endow each generalized state model with a function that selects a set of states as being, intuitively, the set of states that *are the case*. A fact of a generalized state model is said to *obtain* when it contains a state that is the case. Using this notion of fact-obtainment, factive notions of grounding can naturally be defined in terms of the non-factive notions.

---

[29] It can be shown that $\phi \wedge \psi \preccurlyeq \phi$ is logically equivalent to $\psi \preccurlyeq \phi$, and $\phi \wedge \psi \preccurlyeq \psi$ to $\phi \preccurlyeq \psi$. Hence, ∧-Introduction 2 could be simplified to:

$$\frac{\phi \not\preccurlyeq \psi \quad \psi \not\preccurlyeq \phi}{\phi, \psi < \phi \wedge \psi}$$

No such simplification can be made in the case of ∨-Introduction 2.

## 3.2 Correia's 'Grounding and Truth-Functions'

In Correia (2010), I introduce an algebraic semantics for the logic of grounding that is in some respects quite different from Fine's (2012a, 2012b) truthmaker semantics. Yet – somewhat surprisingly – the two approaches turn out to have something deep in common.[30] In order to show this, and before presenting my algebraic semantics, let me first elaborate a bit on Fine's account.

Consider a Finean generalized state frame $\mathfrak{F}$ that is full, that is, whose verification space is the set of all the facts of the frame, with state-fusion operation $\prod$. Let $\sqcap_{\mathfrak{F}}$ be its generalized operation of conjunction on sets of states, $\sqcap_{\mathfrak{F}}$ the corresponding binary operation, and $\sqcup_{\mathfrak{F}}$ its binary disjunction operation on sets of states. Define the binary relations $\leqslant_{\mathfrak{F}}$ of *disjunctive parthood* and $\preccurlyeq_{\mathfrak{F}}$ of *partial disjunctive parthood* between $\mathfrak{F}$'s facts as follows:

(Def-$\leqslant_{\mathfrak{F}}$) $F \leqslant_{\mathfrak{F}} G$ iff$_{df}$ for some fact $H$, $F \sqcup_{\mathfrak{F}} H = G$;
(Def-$\preccurlyeq_{\mathfrak{F}}$) $F \preccurlyeq_{\mathfrak{F}} G$ iff$_{df}$ for some fact $H$, $F \sqcap_{\mathfrak{F}} H \leqslant_{\mathfrak{F}} G$.

One can show that for any facts $F$ and $G$ of the frame, $F \leqslant_{\mathfrak{F}} G$ iff $F \subseteq G$ (the fact that facts are closed under $\prod$ is crucial to establish this), and therefore that $\leqslant_{\mathfrak{F}}$ is coextensive with the frame's weak full grounding relation $\leqslant_{\mathfrak{F}}$ restricted to grounds with just one member. One can also show that $F \preccurlyeq_{\mathfrak{F}} G$ iff $F \preccurlyeq_{\mathfrak{F}} G$, where $\preccurlyeq_{\mathfrak{F}}$ is the frame's weak partial grounding relation (here as well the closure property is crucial). It follows that the frame's strict full grounding relation $<_{\mathfrak{F}}$ can be given the following characterization:

(Char-$<_{\mathfrak{F}}$) $\mathcal{F} <_{\mathfrak{F}} F$ iff $\sqcap_{\mathfrak{F}} \mathcal{F} \leqslant_{\mathfrak{F}} F$ and for no $G \in \mathcal{F}$ does $F \preccurlyeq_{\mathfrak{F}} G$.

As we will see shortly, this is essentially the characterization put forward in Correia (2010).

In Correia (2010), the basic structures invoked in the semantics are tuples $\langle \mathcal{F}, \sqcap, - \rangle$, where $\mathcal{F}$ is a nonempty set, interpreted as a set of facts (these facts play the same semantic role as Fine's facts, see below), $\sqcap$ is a binary operation on $\mathcal{F}$, interpreted as an operation of conjunction, and $-$ a unary operation on $\mathcal{F}$, interpreted as an operation of negation. The two operations are required to satisfy certain principles. Define an operation $\sqcup$ of disjunction on facts in terms of the two primitive operations in the obvious way:

- $F \sqcup G =_{df} -(-F \sqcap -G)$.

The principles that $\sqcap$ and $-$ are required to satisfy are the following ones:

---
[30] I develop the comparison between the two approaches to a significant extent in Correia (2023).

- $-F \neq F$
- $--F = F$
- $F \sqcap F = F$
- $F \sqcap G = G \sqcap F$
- $F \sqcap (G \sqcap H) = (F \sqcap G) \sqcap H$
- $F \sqcup (G \sqcap H) = (F \sqcup G) \sqcap (F \sqcup H)$

(These properties deserve discussion, of course; see below.) I will call such structures *factual structures*.[31]

Given a factual structure $\mathfrak{S}$ with (primitive) conjunction operation $\sqcap$ and (defined) disjunction operation $\sqcup$, a relation $\leq_{\mathfrak{S}}$ of disjunctive parthood and a relation $\preccurlyeq_{\mathfrak{S}}$ of partial disjunctive parthood can be defined as in (Def-$\leq_{\mathfrak{F}}$) and (Def-$\preccurlyeq_{\mathfrak{F}}$) above (I use different symbols in the 2010 paper). On my 2010 approach, (non-factive) strict full grounding is understood as a relation that is characterized exactly as $<_{\mathfrak{F}}$ in (Char-$<_{\mathfrak{F}}$), with two minor provisos: the set of grounds is taken to be non-empty and finite, and generalized fact-conjunction is defined in terms of the binary operator $\sqcap$.[32] Thus, the difference between Fine's approach and mine appears to boil down to this: (a) whereas I take facts to be sui generis entities, Fine's facts are defined as sets of states closed under the operation of state-fusion, (b) whereas I take fact-conjunction as a primitive operation and fact-disjunction as an operation defined in terms of fact-conjunction and fact-negation, Fine's fact-conjunction and fact-disjunction are both defined in terms of state-fusion (and set-theoretic union), and (c) unlike Fine, I do not endow my models with a distinguished set of facts capable of being the semantic values of statements.

Factual structures can be used to interpret various languages. Sequent languages like the one in Fine (2012a) provide straightforward examples. Define a *factual model* for such a language to be a tuple $\langle \mathcal{F}, \sqcap, -, [\,] \rangle$, where $\langle \mathcal{F}, \sqcap, - \rangle$ is a factual structure and $[\,]$ a valuation function that takes each atomic sentence of the language into a member of $\mathcal{F}$. Let $\mathfrak{M} = \langle \mathcal{F}, \sqcap, -, [\,] \rangle$ be an arbitrary factual model and let $\mathfrak{S}$ be the underlying factual structure. $[\,]$ is extended to all basic sentences of the language via the obvious clauses:

- $[\neg \phi] = -[\phi]$
- $[\phi \wedge \psi] = [\phi] \sqcap [\psi]$
- $[\phi \vee \psi] = [\phi] \sqcup [\psi]$

---

[31] What I call 'factual structures' in Correia (2010) have an extra element, which plays a role in the interpretation of factive ground-theoretic operators. More on this later.

[32] The provisos are minor because (i) zero-grounding is controversial and (ii) on the natural extension of the 2010 framework where the grounds are allowed to be infinitely many, a generalized conjunction operation on facts would be taken as a primitive and strict full grounding would still be understood along the lines of (Char-$<_{\mathfrak{F}}$).

If the language contains sequents of type $\Delta < \phi$ with $\Delta$ non-empty and finite, then – in conformity with the previous considerations – we put:

- $\Delta < \phi$ holds in $\mathfrak{M}$ iff $\sqcap[\Delta] \leqslant_{\varepsilon} [\phi]$ and for no $G \in [\Delta]$ does $[\phi] \preccurlyeq_{\varepsilon} G$

($\sqcap$ is to be defined in terms of $\sqcap$ in the obvious way.) On that account, all the introduction and elimination rules mentioned at the end of Section 3.1 are validated, as well as the rules of Fine's PLSFG – namely Cut (<), Non-Circularity (<) and Amalgamation (<). For the other types of Finean sequents, we naturally put:

- $\Delta \leqslant \phi$ holds in $\mathfrak{M}$ iff $\sqcap[\Delta] \leqslant_{\varepsilon} [\phi]$
- $\phi \preccurlyeq \psi$ holds in $\mathfrak{M}$ iff $[\phi] \preccurlyeq_{\varepsilon} [\psi]$
- $\phi < \psi$ holds in $\mathfrak{M}$ iff $[\phi] \preccurlyeq_{\varepsilon} [\psi]$ but not $[\psi] \preccurlyeq_{\varepsilon} [\phi]$

Given these clauses, all the rules of Fine's PLG are validated.

Unlike the languages that have been introduced so far in this and the previous section, the language I focus on in Correia (2010) is not a pure sequent language: it allows the combination of sequents with truth-functional connectives, and quantification into sentential position. More precisely, the vocabulary of the language comprises (i) atomic sentences, (ii) sentential variables, (iii) the classical connectives $\wedge$, $\vee$ and $\neg$, (iv) the sentential existential quantifier $\exists$, (v) the operator $<$ for *factive* strict full grounding (I use another symbol in the paper) and the operator $\approx$ for *factual equivalence* (this is a new notion, but its semantics is straightforward – see below), (vi) the brackets (and). The *basic formulas* are built from the atomic sentences *and the sentential variables* using the classical connectives and the brackets, and the *formulas* of the language are defined as follows:

- The basic formulas are formulas;
- If $\Delta$ is a non-empty finite set of basic formulas and $\phi$ a basic formula, $(\Delta < \phi)$ is a formula[33];
- If $\phi$ and $\psi$ are basic formulas, $(\phi \approx \psi)$ is a formula;
- If $A$ and $B$ are formulas, so are $(A \wedge B)$ and $(A \vee B)$;
- If $A$ is a formula, so is $\neg A$;
- If $A$ is a formula and $x$ a sentential variable, $\exists x A$ is a formula.

Disjunctive parthood and partial disjunctive parthood are definable in the language (with the variable so chosen as to avoid unwanted binding):

---

[33] In the 2010 paper, I take $\Delta$ to be a finite *list* of basic formulas instead, but the difference is immaterial.

- $\phi \leqslant \psi := \exists x((\phi \vee x) \approx \psi)$
- $\phi \preccurlyeq \psi := \exists x((\phi \wedge x) \leqslant \psi)$

I will adopt standard definitions and notational conventions. I will use $\phi \npreccurlyeq \psi$ for $\neg(\phi \preccurlyeq \psi)$, and where $\Delta$ is a non-empty finite set of basic formulas, I will take $\bigwedge \Delta$ to stand for a particular basic formula built from $\Delta$'s members and $\wedge$ such that every member of $\Delta$ appears exactly once in the formula (which formula it is exactly does not matter since all such formulas are logically equivalent from the point of view of the logic to be introduced below).

The language is interpreted by means of factual models as defined above but enriched with a function that selects a set of facts (intuitively: the facts that *obtain*) such that the conjunction of two facts obtain iff both facts obtain, and the negation of a fact obtains iff the fact fails to obtain. The reason why there is this extra element in the models is that, unlike in logics we previously encountered, the basic sentences can be assessed as being true or not true relative to models. Having this extra element allows one to semantically characterize, in addition to a non-factive notion of strict full grounding, a factive notion.

Consider an enriched factual model $\mathfrak{M} = \langle \mathcal{F}, \sqcap, -, ob, [\,] \rangle$, where $ob$ is a subset of $\mathcal{F}$ that represents the set of all the facts that obtain. Where $\rho$ is an assignment of values to the variables and $\phi$ is an atomic sentence or a sentential variable, we let $[\phi]_\rho$ be $[\phi]$ if $\phi$ is an atomic sentence and $\rho(\phi)$ if $\phi$ is a sentential variable. $[\,]_\rho$ is then extended to all basic formulas in the obvious way. The notion of a formula $A$'s *holding* in $\mathfrak{M}$ relative to an assignment of values to the variables $\rho$ – symbolized by $M, \rho \vDash A$ – is defined as follows:

- $M, \rho \vDash \phi$ iff $[\phi]_\rho \in ob$ for $\phi$ a basic formula;
- $M, \rho \vDash \Delta < \phi$ iff (a) $\sqcap [\Delta]_\rho \leqslant_\varepsilon [\phi]_\rho$ and for no $G \in [\Delta]_\rho$ does $[\phi]_\rho \preccurlyeq_\varepsilon G$, and (b) $G \in ob$ for all $G \in [\Delta]_\rho$;
- $M, \rho \vDash \phi \approx \psi$ iff $[\phi]_\rho = [\psi]_\rho$;
- $M, \rho \vDash A \wedge B$ iff $M, \rho \vDash A$ and $M, \rho \vDash B$;
- $M, \rho \vDash A \vee B$ iff $M, \rho \vDash A$ or $M, \rho \vDash B$;
- $M, \rho \vDash \neg A$ iff it is not the case that $M, \rho \vDash A$;
- $M, \rho \vDash \exists x A$ iff $M, \mu \vDash A$ for some assignment $\mu$ that differs from $\rho$ at most on $x$.

We then have:

- $M, \rho \vDash \phi \leqslant \psi$ iff $[\phi]_\rho \leqslant_\varepsilon [\phi]_\rho$;
- $M, \rho \vDash \phi \preccurlyeq \psi$ iff $[\phi]_\rho \preccurlyeq_\varepsilon [\psi]_\rho$.

A formula is said to be *G-valid* iff it is true in all models relative to all assignments to the variables.

Let G be the axiomatic, Hilbert-style system as defined in Figure 6.

System G consists of a classical axiomatic basis for the propositional calculus, plus a suitable axiomatic basis to handle the sentential quantifier, plus the following specific axioms:

*Factual Equivalence*

$\phi \approx \neg\neg\phi$
$\phi \approx \phi \wedge \phi$
$\phi \wedge \psi \approx \psi \wedge \phi$
$\phi \wedge (\psi \wedge \chi) \approx (\phi \wedge \psi) \wedge \chi$
$\phi \vee \psi \approx \neg(\neg\phi \wedge \neg\psi)$
$\phi \vee (\psi \wedge \chi) \approx (\phi \vee \psi) \wedge (\phi \vee \chi)$
$(\phi \approx \psi) \supset (\neg\phi \approx \neg\psi)$
$(\phi \approx \psi) \supset (\phi \wedge \chi \approx \psi \wedge \chi)$
$(\phi \approx \psi) \wedge (\psi \approx \chi) \supset (\phi \approx \chi)$
$(\phi \approx \psi) \supset (\psi \approx \phi)$
$(\phi \approx \psi) \supset (\phi \equiv \psi)$

*Substitution*

$(\Delta < \phi \wedge \phi \approx \psi) \supset \Delta < \psi$
$(\Delta, \phi < \chi \wedge \phi \approx \psi) \supset \Delta, \psi < \chi$

*Structure*

$(\Delta, \phi < \psi \wedge \Gamma < \phi) \supset \Delta, \Gamma < \psi$        Cut
$\neg(\Delta, \phi < \phi)$        Irreflexivity
$\Delta < \phi \supset \bigwedge\Delta \wedge \phi$        Factivity

*Introduction*

$(\Delta < \phi \wedge \Gamma < \psi) \supset \Delta, \Gamma < \phi \wedge \psi$        $\wedge$-Introduction 1
$\Delta < \phi \supset \Delta < \phi \vee \psi$        $\vee$-Introduction 1
$\Delta < \psi \supset \Delta < \phi \vee \psi$
$(\phi \wedge \psi \not\approx \phi \wedge \phi \wedge \psi \not\approx \psi) \supset \phi, \psi < \phi \wedge \psi$        $\wedge$-Introduction 2
$\phi \vee \psi \not\approx \phi \supset \phi < \phi \vee \psi$        $\vee$-Introduction 2
$\phi \vee \psi \not\approx \psi \supset \psi < \phi \vee \psi$

*Elimination*

$\Delta, \phi \wedge \psi < \chi \supset \Delta, \phi, \psi < \chi$        $\wedge$-Elimination
$\Delta, \phi \vee \psi < \chi \supset \Delta, \phi < \chi$        $\vee$-Elimination
$\Delta, \phi \vee \psi < \chi \supset \Delta, \psi < \chi$

*Subsumption*

$\Delta < \phi \supset \bigwedge\Delta \leqslant \phi$

**Figure 6** The system G

Note that whereas the amalgamation principle for < is not expressed by means of an axiom of the system, it is derivable from ∧-Introduction 1, the first substitution principle and the theorem $\phi \wedge \phi \approx \phi$. Since the formulas of type $\Delta < \phi$ are built from finitely many basic formulas, the version of Fine's cut principle for < in the language of G is derivable from G's cut axiom. G's introduction and elimination axioms correspond to the introduction and elimination rules of the same name validated by Fine's (2012a) semantics.[34]

The main result of Correia (2010) is that G is sound and complete with respect to the proposed semantics:

**Theorem 8** (Soundness and completeness for G). *A formula is a theorem of G iff it is G-valid.*

Soundness and completeness are preserved if we remove the Factivity axiom from G and keep only condition (a) in the semantic clause for <.

The logic determined by the axioms for factual equivalence is R. B. Angell's (1977) logic of analytic equivalence. As we will see with some illustrations in Section 4.1, there is room for disagreement about which logic factual equivalence should be taken to have.

Factual equivalence has a distinguished role in system G. Semantically, strict full grounding is definable in terms of fact-disjunction and fact-conjunction, as per the truth-clause for <. This definability is manifest in the object language: where $\bigwedge_{\psi \in \Delta} (\phi \not\preceq \psi)$ stands for a conjunction of the formulas of type $\neg(\phi \preceq \psi)$ with $\psi \in \Delta$ (which conjunction exactly does not matter),

$$\Delta < \phi \equiv \bigwedge \Delta \wedge (\bigwedge \Delta \preceq \phi) \wedge \bigwedge_{\psi \in \Delta} (\phi \not\preceq \psi)$$

is indeed a theorem of G / a G-valid formula. (If < is interpreted as non-factive, just drop the first conjunct.) In Correia (2010), I expressed doubts about the idea that strict full grounding is definable in terms of factual equivalence in that way – more precisely, I expressed doubts about the idea that the Subsumption axiom $\Delta < \phi \supset \bigwedge \Delta \preceq \phi$ should be deemed universally true. But I changed my mind since then: see Correia and Skiles (2019) for a defence of the idea.

---

[34] The antecedent in ∧-Introduction 2 can be simplified to $\phi \not\preceq \psi \wedge \psi \not\preceq \phi$, the antecedent in the first axiom under ∨-Introduction 2 to $\psi \not\preceq \phi$, and the antecedent in the second axiom under ∨-Introduction 2 to $\phi \not\preceq \psi$. The logic of $\preceq$ is thus not exactly the same as the logic of the Finean $\preceq$ (see footnote 29). The difference between the two logics can be seen to ultimately rest on a difference between the way Correia (2010) and Fine (2012a) treat the interaction between fact-conjunction and fact-disjunction: whereas my 2010 semantics takes the latter to distribute over the latter, Fine's (2012a) semantics does not. I will come back to this in Sections 3.3 and 4.1.

## 3.3 Lovett's 'The Logic of Ground'

Lovett (2020a) devises a proof system for the logic of (non-factive) weak full grounding that is inspired by Fine's (2012a) views, and which is closely related to the system G put forward in Correia (2010). Indeed, as Lovett shows, the two systems are 'definitionally equivalent', in a sense I will make precise below.

Lovett's system, LWFG, is a Hilbert-style system formulated in a language that is just like G's language except that (i) it has no quantifiers and no variables and (ii) its sole non-standard operator is the operator $\leqslant$ for weak full grounding, which is given the grammar that $<$ has in G. The system is defined as in Figure 7.

Since $\leqslant$-sequents are built from finitely many basic formulas, the cut axiom could be formulated in the same manner as the cut axiom for $<$ in G: $(\Delta, \phi \leqslant \psi \wedge \Gamma \leqslant \phi) \supset \Delta, \Gamma \leqslant \psi$. Lovett's formulation of the bilateral introduction axiom is (in effect) the more complex $(\phi \leqslant \psi \wedge \psi \leqslant \phi) \supset (\neg \phi \leqslant \neg \psi \wedge \neg \psi \leqslant \neg \phi)$,

---

System LWFG consists of a classical axiomatic basis for the propositional calculus, plus the following specific axioms:

*Structure*

$(\Delta_1 \leqslant \phi_1 \wedge \Delta_2 \leqslant \phi_2 \wedge \ldots \wedge \phi_1, \phi_2, \ldots \leqslant \phi) \supset \Delta_1, \Delta_2, \ldots \leqslant \phi$    Cut
$\phi \leqslant \psi \supset (\phi \supset \psi)$    Implication

*Right-Introduction*

$\phi, \psi \leqslant \phi \wedge \psi$
$\phi \leqslant \phi \vee \psi$
$\psi \leqslant \phi \vee \psi$
$\neg \phi, \neg \psi \leqslant \neg(\phi \vee \psi)$
$\neg \phi \leqslant \neg(\phi \wedge \psi)$
$\neg \psi \leqslant \neg(\phi \wedge \psi)$
$\phi \leqslant \neg\neg \phi$

*Left-Introduction*

$\Delta, \phi, \psi \leqslant \chi \supset \Delta, \phi \wedge \psi \leqslant \chi$
$(\Delta, \phi \leqslant \chi \wedge \Gamma, \psi \leqslant \chi) \supset \Delta, \Gamma, \phi \vee \psi \leqslant \chi$
$\Delta, \neg \phi, \neg \psi \leqslant \chi \supset \Delta, \neg(\phi \vee \psi) \leqslant \chi$
$(\Delta, \neg \phi \leqslant \chi \wedge \Gamma, \neg \psi \leqslant \chi) \supset \Delta, \Gamma, \neg(\phi \wedge \psi) \leqslant \chi$
$\neg\neg \phi \leqslant \phi$

*Bilateral Introduction*

$(\phi \leqslant \psi \wedge \psi \leqslant \phi) \supset \neg \phi \leqslant \neg \psi$

**Figure 7** The system LWFG

but the latter formula is derivable from the bilateral introduction axiom as I formulate it. Lovett adds $\phi \leqslant \phi$ as an axiom to his system, but this is not needed thanks to the cut axiom and axioms $\phi \leqslant \neg\neg\phi$ and $\neg\neg\phi \leqslant \phi$.

Each axiom except for Implication corresponds in an obvious way to a rule of the sort used in the formulation of Fine's logics, that is, rules that licence derivations of one sequent from a collection of zero or more sequents. One can easily verify that the rules distinct from those that correspond to the second and the fourth Left-Introduction axioms and to the Bilateral Introduction axiom are validated by Fine's truthmaker semantics (see Section 3.1). The rule corresponding to the Bilateral Introduction axiom is not validated, and the reason is immediate: there are models where two basic sentences have the same verifiers but not the same falsifiers. The rules that correspond to the second and the fourth Left-Introduction axioms are not validated either.[35] Take the rule that corresponds to the second Left-Introduction axiom as an illustration. Set $\Delta = \varnothing, \Gamma = \{\xi\}$ and $\chi = \phi \vee (\xi \wedge \psi)$. Both $\phi \leqslant \phi \vee (\xi \wedge \psi)$ and $\xi, \psi \leqslant \phi \vee (\xi \wedge \psi)$ are valid (i.e., hold in all models), and so if the Finean semantics validated the rule, $\xi, \phi \vee \psi \leqslant \phi \vee (\xi \wedge \psi)$ would also be valid. But it is not.[36]

These last two rules deserve a bit more discussion. In Fine's truthmaker semantics, $\wedge$ distributes over $\vee$ in the sense that $\phi \wedge (\psi \vee \chi)$ and $(\phi \wedge \psi) \vee (\phi \wedge \chi)$ have the same verifiers in any model. By contrast, $\vee$ does not distribute over $\wedge$: whereas every verifier of $\phi \vee (\psi \wedge \chi)$ is a verifier of $(\phi \vee \psi) \wedge (\phi \vee \chi)$ in every model, there are models where some instances of $(\phi \vee \psi) \wedge (\phi \vee \chi)$ have verifiers that do not verify the corresponding instances of $\phi \vee (\psi \wedge \chi)$.[37] Translated in terms of weak full grounding, the situation can thus be summarized as follows:

- Both $\phi \wedge (\psi \vee \chi) \leqslant (\phi \wedge \psi) \vee (\phi \wedge \chi)$ and its converse $(\phi \wedge \psi) \vee (\phi \wedge \chi) \leqslant \phi \wedge (\psi \vee \chi)$ are valid (i.e., hold in every model).
- Whereas $\phi \vee (\psi \wedge \chi) \leqslant (\phi \vee \psi) \wedge (\phi \vee \chi)$ is valid, its converse $(\phi \vee \psi) \wedge (\phi \vee \chi) \leqslant \phi \vee (\psi \wedge \chi)$ is not.

Now the following can be shown[38]:

---

[35] Interestingly, taking $\Delta = \Gamma$ yields rules that *are* validated in the Finean semantics.
[36] Take $\xi, \phi$ and $\psi$ atomic, and consider a model where $[\xi]^+ = \{s\}, [\phi]^+ = \{t\}$ and $[\psi]^+ = \{u\}$ where $s, t$ and $u$ are distinct and *independent*, where this means that for any non-empty subsets $S$ and $T$ of $\{s, t, u\}$, $S \neq T$ implies $\prod S \neq \prod T$. Then $st$ verifies $\xi \wedge (\phi \vee \psi)$ but not $\phi \vee (\xi \wedge \psi)$, and therefore $\xi, \phi \vee \psi \leqslant \phi \vee (\xi \wedge \psi)$ does not hold in the model.
[37] If $[\phi]^+ = \{s\}, [\psi]^+ = \{t\}$ and $[\chi]^+ = \{u\}$ where $s, t$ and $u$ are distinct and independent, then $[\phi \vee (\psi \wedge \chi)]^+$ is *strictly* included in $[(\phi \vee \psi) \wedge (\phi \vee \chi)]^+$.
[38] (a) 'Only if' direction: Assume that $\Delta, \phi' \leqslant \chi'$ and $\Gamma, \psi' \leqslant \chi'$ both hold in model $\mathfrak{M}$. Then so do $\bigwedge \Delta \wedge \phi' \leqslant \chi'$ and $\bigwedge \Gamma \wedge \psi' \leqslant \chi'$, and hence so does $((\bigwedge \Delta \wedge \phi') \vee (\bigwedge \Gamma \wedge \psi')) \leqslant \chi'$. Given that all the instances of $(\phi \vee \psi) \wedge (\phi \vee \chi) \leqslant \phi \vee (\psi \wedge \chi)$ hold in $\mathfrak{M}$, one can then show that $\bigwedge \Delta \wedge \bigwedge \Gamma \wedge (\phi' \vee \psi') \leqslant \chi'$, and hence $\Delta, \Gamma, \phi' \vee \psi' \leqslant \chi'$, holds in $\mathfrak{M}$. (b) 'If' direction: The following two sequents are valid: $\phi \leqslant \phi \vee (\psi \wedge \chi); \psi, \chi \leqslant \phi \vee (\psi \wedge \chi)$. Given the assumption

# The Logic of Grounding 41

**Proposition 9.** *Let $\mathfrak{M}$ be a Finean model. All the instances of $(\phi \vee \psi) \wedge (\phi \vee \chi) \leqslant \phi \vee (\psi \wedge \chi)$ hold in $\mathfrak{M}$ iff every instance of the rule*

$$\frac{\Delta, \phi' \leqslant \chi' \quad \Gamma, \psi' \leqslant \chi'}{\Delta, \Gamma, \phi' \vee \psi' \leqslant \chi'},$$

*where $\Delta$ and $\Gamma$ are finite, is validated by $\mathfrak{M}$, that is, if its premises hold in $\mathfrak{M}$, then so does its conclusion.*

Since, as I stressed, $(\phi \vee \psi) \wedge (\phi \vee \chi) \leqslant \phi \vee (\psi \wedge \chi)$ is not valid in the Finean semantics, it immediately follows that, as previously announced, the rule corresponding to Lovett's second Left-Introduction is not validated by the semantics. The fact that the rule corresponding to the fourth Left-Introduction is not validated by the semantics can then be easily shown.

Let me now turn to the connection between LWFG and G. In G, fact-disjunction distributes over fact-conjunction as well as vice versa, and so it is natural to suspect that LWFG and G have a lot in common. This is the case, as Lovett shows. In G, the following are theorems (see Correia 2010: 265–6):

- $\phi \leqslant \psi \equiv ((\phi \vee \psi) \approx \psi)$
- $\phi \prec \psi \equiv ((\phi \wedge \psi) \leqslant \psi)$

This implies that $\leqslant$ and $\prec$ could have been defined without using quantifiers. Consider now the system pG, formulated in a language just like G's but without the quantifier and the variables, and axiomatized like G but with the following differences: (i) the postulates for the quantifier are dropped, and, in line with the previous remark, (ii) $\phi \leqslant \psi$ is defined as $(\phi \vee \psi) \approx \psi$ and $\phi \prec \psi$ as $(\phi \wedge \psi) \leqslant \psi$. pG may thus properly be called a propositional version of G. The connection that Lovett establishes is, to be precise, between LWFG and pG.

Assume LWFG and pG are defined on the basis of the same the set of atomic sentences. Define the systems LWFG$^+$ and pG$^+$ as follows:

LWFG$^+$:

- LWFG$^+$'s language is like LWFG's except that it has the two extra operators $\approx$ and $<$ with the same grammar as in pG
- The postulates of LWFG$^+$ are those of LWFG (formulated in LWFG$^+$'s language), plus the following axioms:

$$\phi \approx \psi \equiv (\phi \leqslant \psi \wedge \psi \leqslant \phi)$$

---

on the rule, it follows that $\psi, \phi \vee \chi \leqslant \phi \vee (\psi \wedge \chi)$ holds in $\mathfrak{M}$. Given this and the validity of $\phi \leqslant \phi \vee (\psi \wedge \chi)$, the assumption on the rule yields that $\phi \vee \psi, \phi \vee \chi \leqslant \phi \vee (\psi \wedge \chi)$, and hence $(\phi \vee \psi) \wedge (\phi \vee \chi) \leqslant \phi \vee (\psi \wedge \chi)$, holds in $\mathfrak{M}$.

$$\Delta < \phi \equiv \bigwedge \Delta \wedge (\Delta \leqslant \phi) \wedge \bigwedge_{\psi \in \Delta} (\phi \not\approx \psi)$$

where $\bigwedge_{\psi \in \Delta} (\phi \not\approx \psi)$ stands for a conjunction of the formulas of type $\neg(\phi, \psi \leqslant \psi)$ with $\psi \in \Delta$ (exactly which conjunction does not matter)

pG$^+$:

- pG$^+$'s language is like pG's except that it has the extra operator $\leqslant$ with the same grammar as in LWFG
- The postulates of pG$^+$ are those of pG (formulated in pG$^+$'s language), plus the following axiom:

$$\Delta \leqslant \phi \equiv \bigwedge \Delta \leqslant \phi$$

LWFG$^+$ is thus naturally seen as a system that defines $\approx$ and $<$ in terms of $\leqslant$, and pG$^+$ as a system that defines $\leqslant$ in terms of $\approx$. Lovett establishes, in effect, the following fact:

**Theorem 10.** *LWFG$^+$ and pG$^+$ have exactly the same theorems.*

This is the sense in which LWFG and pG are definitionally equivalent.

Variants of Lovett's result can easily be established. If $<$ is understood as non-factive, the Factivity axiom in the formulation of pG is to be dropped; Theorem 10 still holds if the conjunct $\bigwedge \Delta$ is removed from LWFG$^+$'s second extra axiom. Or start with G instead of its propositional version pG, and with the quantified version of LWFG obtained by adding G's quantificational apparatus (quantifier plus variables plus the relevant postulates) to LWFG. Then Theorem 10 still holds *mutatis mutandis*. Likewise if G's Factivity axiom is dropped and the conjunct $\bigwedge \Delta$ is removed from the definitional axiom for $<$.

## 3.4 Correia's 'A New Semantic Framework for the Logic of Worldly Grounding (and Beyond)'

In Correia (2023), I compare the algebraic semantics of Correia (2010) with the Finean truthmaker semantics as developed in Fine (2012a, 2012b), highlighting what is common to the two semantics as well as what is different. I also argue that each semantics has advantages over the other one, along the following lines (the summary is very rough, the reader should consult the paper for details):

- I argue that it is better to treat negation as a purely linguistic phenomenon, as Fine does, rather than as corresponding to an operation on facts, as I do.
- In my logic, fact-disjunction distributes over fact-conjunction, whereas in Fine's semantics is does not (see the discussion in the previous section). As I

(2016) and Krämer and Roski (2015) independently argued, the distributivity principle conflicts with certain intuitive views about grounding (I will come back to this in Section 4.1). Hence, the Finean semantics score points in this respect.

- In Fine's semantics, each fact has disjunctive parts which are disjunctively atomic, that is, disjunctive parts that have no proper disjunctive parts, and I argue that this rules out certain coherent views regarding what grounds what. Here it is my algebraic semantics which scores points, since it leaves room for facts without disjunctively atomic disjunctive parts.
- In Fine's semantics, disjunctive parthood satisfies the principle of Weak Supplementation (if $F$ has a proper disjunctive part $G$, then it also has a disjunctive part $H$ such that $G$ and $H$ do not disjunctively overlap, that is, such that $G$ and $H$ do not share a disjunctive part), and I argue that this rules out certain coherent views regarding what grounds what. My algebraic semantics scores points once again, since it does not force disjunctive parthood to satisfy Weak Supplementation.

And I finally raise an objection to both semantics – or rather, to Fine's semantics and to the natural extension of my semantics that accommodates infinite disjunctions of facts: they countenance a disjunctively universal fact in every model, that is, a fact that has all the facts as disjunctive parts, and there are reasons to deny that there are such facts.[39]

In light of these considerations, I put forward a new, 'best of both worlds' semantic framework, one that is in the spirit of what is common to the Finean semantics and my algebraic semantics but which escapes the various criticisms that I have just listed. The basic structures that I invoke are triples $\langle \mathcal{F}, \sqcap, \sqcup \rangle$, where $\mathcal{F}$ (facts) is a non-empty set, and $\sqcap$ (conjunction) and $\sqcup$ (disjunction) are (not necessarily total) mappings from subsets of $\mathcal{F}$ to $\mathcal{F}$. For some applications – in particular if one wants to semantically characterize factive notions of grounding – one may add an element that specifies which facts of the structure obtain, as in the structures used in Correia (2010). Which conditions conjunction and disjunction should be taken to satisfy in such structures is to a large extent open for discussion, but some conditions seem to impose themselves, such as for instance:

- $\sqcap$ and $\sqcup$ are defined on the very same sets of facts
- For all facts $F$, $\sqcap$ and $\sqcup$ are defined on $\{F\}$, and $\sqcap\{F\} = \sqcup\{F\} = F$

---

[39] In response to my objections to his semantics, Fine (2023) invokes a possible extension of his semantics where disjunctive *states* are allowed and exploits the fact that the verification space of a generalized state model need not be the set of all facts. Space is lacking for a proper discussion of these moves.

Given my purposes in the paper, I focus on structures in which the operations satisfying the conditions just mentioned plus the following conditions on any family $(\mathcal{F}_1, \mathcal{F}_2, \ldots)$ of sets of facts for which the relevant conjunctions / disjunctions exist:

- $\sqcap\{\sqcap \mathcal{F}_1, \sqcap \mathcal{F}_2, \ldots\} = \sqcap\{\mathcal{F}_1 \cup \mathcal{F}_2 \cup \ldots\}$     Associativity ($\sqcap$)
- $\sqcup\{\sqcup \mathcal{F}_1, \sqcup \mathcal{F}_2, \ldots\} = \sqcup\{\mathcal{F}_1 \cup \mathcal{F}_2 \cup \ldots\}$     Associativity ($\sqcup$)
- $\sqcap\{\sqcup \mathcal{F}_1, \sqcup \mathcal{F}_2, \ldots\} = \sqcup\{\sqcap \mathcal{G}_a, \sqcap \mathcal{G}_b, \ldots\}$
  where $\mathcal{G}_a, \mathcal{G}_b, \ldots$ are all the selections from $\{\mathcal{F}_1, \mathcal{F}_2, \ldots\}$     Distributivity ($\sqcap/\sqcup$)

Given a structure $\mathfrak{S} = \langle \mathcal{F}, \sqcap, \sqcup \rangle$ as initially characterized, disjunctive parthood ($\leqslant_\mathfrak{S}$), partial disjunctive parthood ($\preccurlyeq_\mathfrak{S}$), (non-factive) weak full grounding ($\leqslant_\mathfrak{S}$) and (non-factive) weak partial grounding ($\preccurlyeq_\mathfrak{S}$) are naturally defined as follows:

- $F \leqslant_\mathfrak{S} G$ iff$_{df}$ for some $\mathcal{G} \subseteq \mathcal{F}$ such that $F \in \mathcal{G}$, $\sqcup \mathcal{G}$ exists and $\sqcup \mathcal{G} = G$
- $F \preccurlyeq_\mathfrak{S} G$ iff$_{df}$ for some $\mathcal{G} \subseteq \mathcal{F}$ such that $F \in \mathcal{G}$, $\sqcap \mathcal{G}$ exists and $\sqcap \mathcal{G} \leqslant G$
- $\mathcal{G} \leqslant_\mathfrak{S} F$ iff$_{df}$ $\sqcap \mathcal{G}$ exists and $\sqcap \mathcal{G} \leqslant_\mathfrak{S} F$
- $F \preccurlyeq_\mathfrak{S} G$ iff$_{df}$ for some $\mathcal{G} \subseteq \mathcal{F}$ such that $F \in \mathcal{G}$, $\mathcal{G} \leqslant_\mathfrak{S} G$

Of course, $\preccurlyeq_\mathfrak{S}$ and $\preccurlyeq_\mathfrak{S}$ are coextensive. With these relations in place, one can define a relation of (non-factive) strict full grounding ($<_\mathfrak{S}$) in the Fine (2012a/b)-Correia (2010) spirit, either in Finean letter:

- $\mathcal{G} <_\mathfrak{S} F$ iff$_{df}$ $\mathcal{G} \leqslant_\mathfrak{S} F$ and for no $G \in \mathcal{G}$ is it the case that $F \preccurlyeq_\mathfrak{S} G$

or, equivalently, in Correian letter:

- $\mathcal{G} <_\mathfrak{S} F$ iff$_{df}$ $\sqcap \mathcal{G} \leqslant_\mathfrak{S} F$ and for no $G \in \mathcal{G}$ is it the case that $F \preccurlyeq_\mathfrak{S} G$

It is then obvious how the ground-theoretic languages described in previous sections can be interpreted using the structures under consideration, in line with the Finean treatment of negation: endow each structure with two interpretation functions $[\ ]^+$ and $[\ ]^-$, each function associating a fact of the structure to each atomic sentence of the language, and provide the relevant semantic clause for each operator / quantifier of the language.

In Correia (2023), I semantically characterize three systems in the new framework, two systems for factual equivalence (see footnote 48) and one system for (non-factive) weak full grounding. Let me here I present the latter system. The language of the system is like the Finean language of Section 3.1 except that (i) it has only one ground-theoretic operator, $\leqslant$, and sequents of type $\varnothing \leqslant \phi$ are ignored, and (ii) instead of having the standard binary conjunction and disjunction operators, the language has a generalized conjunction operator

*Structure*

$$\frac{\Delta_1 \leqslant \phi_1 \quad \Delta_2 \leqslant \phi_2 \quad \ldots \quad \phi_1, \phi_2, \ldots \leqslant \phi}{\Delta_1, \Delta_2, \ldots \leqslant \phi} \qquad \text{Cut } (\leqslant)$$

*Right-Introduction*

$$\overline{\Delta \leqslant \bigwedge \Delta}$$

$$\overline{\phi \leqslant \bigvee \Delta} \quad \phi \in \Delta$$

$$\overline{\neg \Delta \leqslant \neg \bigvee \Delta}$$

$$\overline{\neg \phi \leqslant \neg \bigwedge \Delta} \quad \phi \in \Delta$$

$$\overline{\phi \leqslant \neg\neg \phi}$$

*Left-Introduction*

$$\frac{\Delta_1, \Delta_2, \ldots \leqslant \phi}{\bigwedge \Delta_1, \bigwedge \Delta_2, \ldots \leqslant \phi}$$

$$\frac{\Gamma_a \leqslant \phi \quad \Gamma_b \leqslant \phi \quad \ldots}{\bigvee \Delta_1, \bigvee \Delta_2, \ldots \leqslant \phi} \qquad \Gamma_a, \Gamma_b, \ldots = \text{all the selections from } \{\Delta_1, \Delta_2, \ldots\}$$

$$\frac{\neg \Delta_1, \neg \Delta_2, \ldots \leqslant \phi}{\neg \bigvee \Delta_1, \neg \bigvee \Delta_2, \ldots \leqslant \phi}$$

$$\frac{\Gamma_a \leqslant \phi \quad \Gamma_b \leqslant \phi \quad \ldots}{\neg \bigwedge \Delta_1, \neg \bigwedge \Delta_2, \ldots \leqslant \phi} \qquad \Gamma_a, \Gamma_b, \ldots = \text{all the selections from } \{\neg \Delta_1, \neg \Delta_2, \ldots\}$$

$$\overline{\neg\neg \phi \leqslant \phi}$$

**Figure 8** Rules for ILWFG

$\bigwedge$ and a generalized disjunction operator $\bigvee$, each being able to take a set $\Delta$ of one, two or more basic formulas to make a further basic formula – $\bigwedge \Delta$ or $\bigvee \Delta$, depending on the case. The models for this language are the models described above in which conjunction and disjunction operate on all and only the non-empty sets of facts. The system is, like PLG and other systems previously discussed, a system for deriving sequents from sets of sequents. Where $\Delta$ is a set of basic formulas, let $\neg \Delta$ be the set of all formulas $\neg \phi$ for $\phi \in \Delta$. The rules of the system – which I will call here 'ILWFG' ('I' is for 'infinitary') – are listed in Figure 8.

Given Cut ($\leqslant$) and the two rules which feature $\neg\neg$, the Identity rule (which states that $\phi \leqslant \phi$ may be inferred no matter what) is derivable. Interestingly, given Cut and the first four Right-Introduction rules, the first four Left-Introduction rules are *revertible*: for each of these rules, one can prove the premiss(es) starting from the conclusion. Also, given Cut, one can derive the first four Right-Introduction rules if we assume the reversed versions of the first four Left-Introduction rules. This means that one could axiomatize the system using the latter instead of the former.[40]

In Correia (2023), I establish the adequacy of ILWFG with respect to the proposed semantics:

**Theorem 11** (Soundness and completeness for ILWFG). *A sequent $\sigma$ is derivable from a set of sequents $\Sigma$ in ILWFG iff $\sigma$ holds in every model (of the sort introduced above) in which the members of $\Sigma$ hold.*

Fine's operators of conjunction and disjunction on facts satisfy the conditions imposed on fact-conjunction and fact-disjunction in the proposed semantics. It follows that the proposed system is also sound with respect the Finean semantics – that is, given the appropriate interpretation of the language of the system within that semantics. I do not know whether it is complete.

System ILWFG is importantly different from Lovett's LWFG. Of course, the language of LWFG has binary conjunction and disjunction rather than the generalized operators of ILWFG's language, and LWFG's sequents are all built from finitely many basic sentences. But there is a deeper difference. System LWFG's axioms correspond to rules that are derivable in ILWFG, except for the rules corresponding to LWFG's second and fourth Left-Introduction axioms and to its Bilateral Introduction axiom. In this respect, ILWFG sides with the logic determined by Fine's truthmaker semantics. This is of course not surprising in light of the discussion in Section 3.3, given that (i) the semantics for ILWFG deals with negation in the same way as Fine's truthmaker semantics does, and (ii) on the semantics for ILWFG as well as on Fine's semantics, fact-disjunction does not distribute over fact-conjunction in all models.

## 3.5 Fine's 'Guide to Ground' (Proof-Theoretic Side) and Correia's 'An Impure Logic of Representational Grounding'

Consider the introduction rules for strict full grounding listed in Figure 9, which Fine (2012a) puts forward.

As I pointed out in Section 3.1, these rules are at odds with the semantics he develops in the same paper: no sequent of type $\phi < \phi \wedge \phi$, $\phi < \phi \vee \phi$, $\neg \phi < \neg(\phi \wedge \phi)$, $\neg \phi < \neg(\phi \vee \phi)$ or $\phi < \neg\neg \phi$ holds in a model. The same is true on *all* the approaches to the impure logic of grounding previously discussed. What are we to do with these rules?

---

[40] I overlooked these last points in Correia (2023).

$$\frac{\phi, \psi < \phi \wedge \psi}{\neg \phi < \neg(\phi \wedge \psi)} \qquad \frac{\phi < \phi \vee \psi}{\neg \psi < \neg(\phi \wedge \psi)} \qquad \frac{\psi < \phi \vee \psi}{\neg \phi, \neg \psi < \neg(\phi \vee \psi)}$$

$$\frac{}{\phi < \neg\neg\phi}$$

**Figure 9** Fine's (2012a) introduction rules for $<$

One option is of course to say that they have to be rejected. But a more plausible view is that they are unproblematic if they are understood as concerning a notion of grounding that is distinct from the notion that Fine's (2012a) semantics – and the logics in Correia (2010), Lovett (2020a) and Correia (2023), for that matter – aimed to capture. I like to put the contrast between the two notions as a contrast between *worldly* notions and *representational* notions of grounding. Roughly put, a notion of grounding is worldly if it is sensitive only to how the world is and not to factors that merely have to do with how the world is represented; and a notion of grounding is representational if, by contrast, it is sensitive to merely representational factors (see Correia 2020; I will elaborate on the distinction in Section 4.1). The difference between, say, any instance of $\phi$ and the corresponding instance of $\phi \wedge \phi$ is purely representational: both sentences, if they represent the world as being some way, represent it as being the same way. Or so it is plausible to claim. If this is correct, then granted that $<$ expresses a worldly notion of grounding and that it is irreflexive, no sequent of type $\phi < \phi \wedge \phi$ can be true. By contrast, if $<$ expresses a representational notion, then it may well be that some, or even all, sequents of type $\phi < \phi \wedge \phi$ are true. The view I am suggesting is that the introduction rules above are suited for some representational notion(s) of strict full grounding.

In addition to these introduction rules, Fine (2012a) lays down elimination rules. One of them has a form we are already familiar with, but the other ones have (except in degenerate cases) disjunctive conclusions. These rules have the following general form, where $\Sigma$, $T_1$, $T_2$, ... are sets of sequents:

$$\frac{\Sigma}{T_1 \mid T_2 \mid \ldots}$$

Such a rule 'says' that from the assumption that all the sequents in $\Sigma$ hold, one may infer that all the sequents in some $T_i$ hold. We may take rules of the form

$$\frac{\Sigma}{T}$$

$$\frac{\Delta < \phi \wedge \psi}{\Delta^1_\phi \leqslant \phi \ \ \Delta^1_\psi \leqslant \psi \ \ | \ \ \Delta^2_\phi \leqslant \phi \ \ \Delta^2_\psi \leqslant \psi \ \ | \ \ \ldots}$$

$$\frac{\Delta < \phi \vee \psi}{\Delta \leqslant \phi \ \ | \ \ \Delta \leqslant \psi \ \ | \ \ \Delta < \phi \wedge \psi}$$

$$\frac{\Delta < \neg(\phi \wedge \psi)}{\Delta \leqslant \neg\phi \ \ | \ \ \Delta \leqslant \neg\psi \ \ | \ \ \Delta < \neg(\phi \vee \psi)}$$

$$\frac{\Delta < \neg(\phi \vee \psi)}{\Delta^1_\phi \leqslant \neg\phi \ \ \Delta^1_\psi \leqslant \neg\psi \ \ | \ \ \Delta^2_\phi \leqslant \neg\phi \ \ \Delta^2_\psi \leqslant \neg\psi \ \ | \ \ \ldots}$$

$$\frac{\Delta < \neg\neg\phi}{\Delta \leqslant \phi}$$

**Figure 10** Fine's (2012a) elimination rules for $<$

to be of the previous form but with only one disjunct in the conclusion. On that account, the rules we have been dealing with previously can be seen as rules of the above general form but with only one disjunct in the conclusion, this disjunct being a singleton. The elimination rules proposed by Fine are as displayed in Figure 10, where the pairs $\langle \Delta^1_\phi, \Delta^1_\psi \rangle, \langle \Delta^2_\phi, \Delta^2_\psi \rangle, \ldots$ are all the pairs $\langle \Delta_a, \Delta_b \rangle$ such that $\Delta_a \cup \Delta_b = \Delta$.

In Correia (2017), I set myself the task of devising a system which comprises the Finean introduction and elimination rules that I have just presented and of devising a semantics relative to which the system is sound and complete. The language of the system is a sequent language with the following types of sequents, where $\Delta$ is a set of basic sentences and $\phi$ a basic sentence:

$\Delta < \phi$
$\Delta \leqslant \phi$
$\Delta \approx \phi$
$\Delta \not< \phi$
$\Delta \not\leqslant \phi$
$\Delta \not\approx \phi$

$<$ is intended to express a non-factive notion of strict full grounding, $\leqslant$ a non-factive notion of weak full grounding, and $\approx$ a notion of propositional equivalence. (I use 'propositional equivalence' rather than 'factual equivalence' in order to emphasize the representational character of the ground-theoretic notions involved in the system.) The intended meanings of the other three operators are the obvious ones. The syntax of $\approx$ is significantly different from the one it had in the language of system G (see Section 3.2). $\Delta \approx \phi$ is intended to mean that (Δ is non-empty and) all the members of Δ are propositionally equivalent to $\phi$. The rules of the system – that I will call 'ILFG', for 'impure logic of full grounding' – are as displayed in Figure 11.

The definitive rules for $\leqslant$ state, in effect, that $\leqslant$ is definable in terms of $<$ and $\approx$, along the following lines: $\Delta \leqslant \phi$ iff$_{df}$ $\Delta \approx \phi$ or $\Delta < \phi$ or $\Delta_1 \approx \phi$ and $\Delta_2 < \phi$ for some $\Delta_1, \Delta_2$ such that $\Delta_1 \cup \Delta_2 = \Delta$.

Due to the peculiar shape of some of the rules, viz. the ones with disjunctive conclusions, the notion of derivability cannot be defined in the same way as in Section 3.1. Let us represent the disjunctive item $T_1 \mid T_2 \mid \ldots$ by the set $\{T_1, T_2, \ldots\}$, and call such sets *requirements*. The relevant notion of derivability is that of a requirement being derivable from a set of sequents. A requirement R *generates* a requirement S iff every member of R contains (as a subset) some member of S. We say that $\{T_1, T_2, \ldots\}$ is *derivable* from $\Sigma$ iff there is a proof of a requirement that generates $\{T_1, T_2, \ldots\}$ from a subset of $\Sigma$. A *proof* of a requirement $\{T_1, T_2, \ldots\}$ from a set of sequents $\Sigma$ is a labelled tree without infinite branches with top $\{T_1, T_2, \ldots\}$ and bottom $\Sigma$, such that each transition from the occupant of a parent node to the occupants of the corresponding children is licensed by one or more (possibly infinitely many) applications of a given rule (see Correia 2017 for a precise definition).[41]

The semantics is of the same general spirit as deRosset's (2015) and Litland's (2018a) graph-theoretic semantics: each model specifies in a somewhat direct way links of strict full grounding between contents – which I call 'propositions' rather than 'facts'. But there is a big difference: the semantics identifies a set of 'simple' propositions, and it initially only specifies what grounds these propositions – what grounds the other propositions being then defined recursively on that basis. Let me be more precise.

Let a *propositional structure* be a tuple $\langle P, \sqcap, \sqcup, - \rangle$ where $P$ (propositions) is a non-empty set, $\sqcap$ (conjunction) and $\sqcup$ (disjunction) are binary operations on $P$, and $-$ (negation) is a unary operation on $P$. A proposition in a propositional structure is

- *negative* iff it is the negation of some proposition
- *conjunctive* iff it is the conjunction of a pair of propositions
- *disjunctive* iff it is the disjunction of a pair of propositions
- *atomic* iff it is neither conjunctive, nor disjunctive, nor negative
- *simple* iff it is atomic or the negation of an atomic proposition

A propositional structure $\langle P, \sqcap, \sqcup, - \rangle$ is *representational* iff the following conditions are satisfied:

---

[41] In the paper, I wrote 'of finite height' instead of 'without infinite branches', but the intention was to mean the absence of infinite branches.

*Structural rules for $\approx$*

$$\frac{}{\phi \approx \phi} \qquad \frac{\phi \approx \psi}{\psi \approx \phi} \qquad \frac{\phi \approx \psi \quad \psi \approx \chi}{\phi \approx \chi}$$

$$\frac{\phi_1 \approx \phi \quad \phi_2 \approx \phi \quad \ldots}{\phi_1, \phi_2, \ldots \approx \phi} \qquad \frac{\phi, \Delta \approx \psi}{\phi \approx \psi} \qquad \frac{\varnothing \approx \phi}{\bot}$$

*Introduction rules for $\approx$*

$$\frac{}{\phi \wedge \psi \approx \psi \wedge \phi} \qquad \frac{}{\phi \vee \psi \approx \psi \vee \phi}$$

$$\frac{\phi \approx \psi}{\phi \wedge \theta \approx \psi \wedge \theta} \qquad \frac{\phi \approx \psi}{\phi \vee \theta \approx \psi \vee \theta} \qquad \frac{\phi \approx \psi}{\neg \phi \approx \neg \psi}$$

*Elimination rules for $\approx$*

$$\frac{\psi \approx \phi \wedge \chi}{\bot} \quad \text{where } \psi \text{ is non-conjunctive}$$

$$\frac{\psi \approx \phi \vee \chi}{\bot} \quad \text{where } \psi \text{ is non-disjunctive}$$

$$\frac{\psi \approx \neg \phi}{\bot} \quad \text{where } \psi \text{ is non-negative}$$

$$\frac{\phi \wedge \psi \approx \phi' \wedge \psi'}{\phi \approx \phi' \quad \psi \approx \psi' \quad | \quad \phi \approx \psi' \quad \psi \approx \phi'}$$

$$\frac{\phi \vee \psi \approx \phi' \vee \psi'}{\phi \approx \phi' \quad \psi \approx \psi' \quad | \quad \phi \approx \psi' \quad \psi \approx \phi'}$$

$$\frac{\neg \phi \approx \neg \psi}{\phi \approx \psi}$$

*Structural rules for $<$*

$$\frac{\Delta_1 < \phi_1 \quad \Delta_2 < \phi_2 \quad \ldots \quad \phi_1, \phi_2, \ldots, \Gamma < \psi}{\Delta_1, \Delta_2, \ldots, \Gamma < \psi} \qquad \text{Cut } (<)$$

$$\frac{\Delta, \phi < \phi}{\bot} \qquad \text{Non-Circularity } (<)$$

$$\frac{\Delta_1 < \phi \quad \Delta_2 < \phi \quad \ldots}{\Delta_1, \Delta_2, \ldots < \phi} \qquad \text{Amalgamation } (<)$$

$$\frac{\Delta < \phi \quad \phi \approx \psi}{\Delta < \psi}$$

$$\frac{\phi_1, \phi_2, \ldots < \psi \quad \psi_1 \approx \phi_1 \quad \psi_2 \approx \phi_2 \quad \ldots}{\psi_1, \psi_2, \ldots < \psi}$$

**Figure 11** Rules for ILFG

*Definitive rules for $\leqslant$*

$$\frac{\Delta \approx \phi}{\Delta \leqslant \phi} \qquad \frac{\Delta < \phi}{\Delta \leqslant \phi} \qquad \frac{\Delta_1 \approx \phi \quad \Delta_2 < \phi}{\Delta_1, \Delta_2 \leqslant \phi}$$

$$\frac{\Delta \leqslant \phi}{\Delta \approx \phi \mid \Delta < \phi \mid \Delta^1_\approx \approx \phi \ \Delta^1_< < \phi \mid \Delta^2_\approx \approx \phi \ \Delta^2_< < \phi \mid \ldots}$$

where the pairs $\langle \Delta^1_\approx, \Delta^1_< \rangle, \langle \Delta^2_\approx, \Delta^2_< \rangle, \ldots$ are all the pairs $\langle \Delta_a, \Delta_b \rangle$ such that $\Delta_a \cup \Delta_b = \Delta$.

*Introduction rules for $<$*

See Figure 9

*Elimination rules for $<$*

See Figure 10

*Complexity rule*

$$\frac{\Delta < \phi}{\bot} \quad \text{where } \phi \text{ is a literal and some member of } \Delta \text{ is not}$$

*Non-Contradiction and Excluded Middle*

$$\frac{\Delta \approx \phi \quad \Delta \not\approx \phi}{\bot} \qquad \frac{\Delta < \phi \quad \Delta \not< \phi}{\bot} \qquad \frac{\Delta \leqslant \phi \quad \Delta \not\leqslant \phi}{\bot}$$

$$\overline{\Delta \approx \phi \mid \Delta \not\approx \phi} \qquad \overline{\Delta < \phi \mid \Delta \not< \phi} \qquad \overline{\Delta \leqslant \phi \mid \Delta \not\leqslant \phi}$$

**Figure 11** (continued)

- Being negative, being conjunctive and being disjunctive are pairwise incompatible properties of propositions
- $\sqcap$ and $\sqcup$ are commutative
- If $P \sqcap Q = P' \sqcap Q'$, then either $P = P'$ and $Q = Q'$ or $P = Q'$ and $Q = P'$
- If $P \sqcup Q = P' \sqcup Q'$, then either $P = P'$ and $Q = Q'$ or $P = Q'$ and $Q = P'$
- If $-P = -Q$, then $P = Q$

And it is *regular* iff it is representational and its set of propositions is generated by the set of its atomic propositions via $\sqcap$, $\sqcup$, and $-$.

Let a *ground-theoretic structure* be a tuple $\mathfrak{S} = \langle P, \sqcap, \sqcup, -, <^0 \rangle$, where $\langle P, \sqcap, \sqcup, - \rangle$ is a regular propositional structure and $<^0$ (strict full grounding) is a relation between sets of propositions and *simple* propositions that satisfies the following conditions:

- If $\mathcal{P}_1 <^0 \mathcal{P}_1, \mathcal{P}_2 <^0 \mathcal{P}_2, \ldots$ and $\mathcal{P}_1, \mathcal{P}_2, \ldots, \mathcal{P} <^0 Q$,

  then $\mathcal{P}_1, \mathcal{P}_2, \ldots, \mathcal{P} <^0 Q$      Cut

- If $\mathcal{P} <^0 P$, then $\mathcal{P} \not\ni P$      Irreflexivity

- If $\mathcal{P}_1 <^0 P$, $\mathcal{P}_2 <^0 P$, ..., then $\mathcal{P}_1, \mathcal{P}_2, \ldots <^0 P$      Amalgamation
- If $\mathcal{P} <^0 P$, then all the members of $\mathcal{P}$ are simple      Complexity

A weak companion $\leqslant^0$ of $<^0$ is defined as follows:

- $\mathcal{P} \leqslant^0 P$ iff$_{df}$ $\mathcal{P} = \{P\}$, or $\mathcal{P} <^0 P$, or for some $\mathcal{P}'$ such that $\mathcal{P} = \{P\} \cup \mathcal{P}'$, $\mathcal{P}' <^0 P$

The propositions in a regular propositional structure are very similar to the formulas of a classical propositional language, and can be assigned degrees of complexity in just the same ways. This makes it possible to recursively extend $<^0$ and $\leqslant^0$ to relations $<^\omega$ and $\leqslant^\omega$ between sets of propositions and *arbitrary* propositions. I skip the details but nevertheless mention that $<^\omega$, just like $<^0$, satisfies Cut, Irreflexivity and Amalgamation, and that the following principles hold:

- $\mathcal{P} \leqslant^\omega P$ iff $\mathcal{P} = \{P\}$, or $\mathcal{P} <^\omega P$, or for some $\mathcal{P}'$ such that $\mathcal{P} = \{P\} \cup \mathcal{P}'$, $\mathcal{P}' <^\omega P$
- $\mathcal{P} <^\omega P \sqcap Q$ iff for some $\mathcal{P}_1, \mathcal{P}_2$ with $\mathcal{P} = \mathcal{P}_1 \cup \mathcal{P}_2$, $\mathcal{P}_1 \leqslant^\omega P$ and $\mathcal{P}_2 \leqslant^\omega Q$
- $\mathcal{P} <^\omega P \sqcup Q$ iff $\mathcal{P} \leqslant^\omega P$ or $\mathcal{P} \leqslant^\omega Q$ or $\mathcal{P} <^\omega P \sqcap Q$
- $\mathcal{P} <^\omega -(P \sqcap Q)$ iff $\mathcal{P} \leqslant^\omega -P$ or $\mathcal{P} \leqslant^\omega -Q$ or $\mathcal{P} <^\omega -(P \sqcup Q)$
- $\mathcal{P} <^\omega -(P \sqcup Q)$ iff for some $\mathcal{P}_1, \mathcal{P}_2$ with $\mathcal{P} = \mathcal{P}_1 \cup \mathcal{P}_2$, $\mathcal{P}_1 \leqslant^\omega -P$ and $\mathcal{P}_2 \leqslant^\omega -Q$
- $\mathcal{P} <^\omega --P$ iff $\mathcal{P} \leqslant^\omega P$

Let a *ground-theoretic model* be a ground-theoretic structure endowed with an interpretation function, which assigns an atomic proposition of the structure to each atomic sentence of the language. Given a ground-theoretic model $\mathfrak{M}$ with interpretation function $[\,]$, $[\,]$ is extended to all basic sentences of the language in the obvious way (put $[\phi \wedge \psi] = [\phi] \sqcap [\psi]$ and so on), and where $<^\omega$ and $\leqslant^\omega$ are the extended strict and weak grounding relation of the underlying structure, respectively, we put:

- $\Delta < \phi$ holds in $\mathfrak{M}$ iff $[\Delta] <^\omega [\phi]$
- $\Delta \leqslant \phi$ holds in $\mathfrak{M}$ iff $[\Delta] \leqslant^\omega [\phi]$
- $\Delta \approx \phi$ holds in $\mathfrak{M}$ iff $[\Delta] = [\phi]$
- $\Delta \not< \phi$ holds in $\mathfrak{M}$ iff $\Delta < \phi$ does not hold in $\mathfrak{M}$
- $\Delta \not\leqslant \phi$ holds in $\mathfrak{M}$ iff $\Delta \leqslant \phi$ does not hold in $\mathfrak{M}$
- $\Delta \not\approx \phi$ holds in $\mathfrak{M}$ iff $\Delta \approx \phi$ does not hold in $\mathfrak{M}$

A requirement $\{T_1, T_2, \ldots\}$ is an *ILFG-consequence* of a set of sequents $\Sigma$ iff for every ground-theoretic model $\mathfrak{M}$ in which all the members of $\Sigma$ hold, there is an $i$ such that all the members of $T_i$ hold in $\mathfrak{M}$.

In the paper, I establish the adequacy of ILFG with respect to the proposed semantics:

**Theorem 12** (Soundness and completeness for ILFG). *A requirement $\{T_1, T_2, \ldots\}$ is derivable from a set of sequents $\Sigma$ in ILFG iff $\{T_1, T_2, \ldots\}$ is an ILFG-consequence of $\Sigma$.*

Propositional equivalence as characterized by ILFG is *very* fine grained, perhaps too fine-grained even for many friends of representational grounding. Another likely target of criticism is the complexity rule, at least if the rule is intended to concern a notion of *metaphysical* grounding. In the paper, I am explicit that < is intended to express such a notion, and I try to defend the complexity rule against objections; but the defence may not convince every sceptic. The rule bears some resemblance to Bolzano's principle that grounded truths cannot be less complex than their grounds (1837: II, §221). Bolzano states this principle for what he calls 'conceptual truths'. Some might wish to argue that my complexity rule is likewise to be restricted to certain kinds of ground-theoretic connections, say to connections of logical grounding.

### 3.6 deRosset and Fine's 'A Semantics for the Impure Logic of Ground'

Impure logic of full grounding embodies a definite conception of propositional equivalence – as I have just stressed, one that is very fine-grained. This contrasts with deRosset and Fine's (2023) impure logic of grounding: the logic is intended to be a 'minimal' logic, that can be enriched in various ways so as to capture various conceptions of propositional equivalence, all quite fine-grained but to various degrees.

Their minimal system, which they call 'GG', is roughly Fine's (2012b) pure logic of grounding PLG (see Figure 1) plus the introduction and elimination rules put forward in Fine (2012a) and appearing in ILFG (see Figures 9 and 10). The qualification 'roughly' is important because there are subtle yet important differences between this description of GG and a properly accurate description of the system. Let me be more precise.

The following two points mark important formal differences between GG on one hand, and PLG and ILFG on the other hand:

(1) In PLG, derivability is of a sequent from a set of sequents. Since some elimination rules for < involve disjunctive conclusions, enriching PLG with these rules forces one to invoke a different kind of derivability relation. In ILFG, derivability is of a *requirement* from a set of sequent, where requirements behave like *disjunctions of conjunctions*: a requirement $\{T_1, T_2, \ldots\}$

holds just in case for some $i$, all the members of $T_i$ hold. GG's derivability relation could be taken to be of the same sort, but deRosset and Fine adopt a slightly simpler option and take the derivability relation of be a relation between two sets of sequents, where one is treated conjunctively, as in PLG and ILFG, and the other one disjunctively: the semantic counterpart of the claim that set of sequents T is derivable from set of sequents $\Sigma$ is the claim that whenever all the members of $\Sigma$ hold, at least one member of T holds. Adopting their approach instead of the approach I adopted in the formulation of ILFG involves no loss (or gain): any principle to the effect that a requirement $\{T_1, T_2, \ldots\}$ follows from a set of sequents $\Sigma$ can be replaced without loss (or gain) by the principle that for any selection T from $\{T_1, T_2, \ldots\}$, T follows from $\Sigma$. (And conversely, the deRosset and Fine derivability relation could be used instead of the one I used in order to characterize ILFG, without any loss or gain.)

(2) Instead of defining derivability in terms of proofs of a set of sequents from a set of sequents (which would be to follow the pattern exemplified in PLG and ILFG), deRosset and Fine introduce a new symbol $\Vdash$ for derivability and devise a system of rules for deriving expressions of type $\Sigma \Vdash T$ – read: set of sequent T is derivable from set of sequents $\Sigma$ – from (possibly empty) sets of such expressions. The formulation of the system thus involves a meta-notion of derivability which is of the same formal kind as the notion of derivability at work in PLG: in both cases, derivability is always of one item from a set of items of the same sort, and it is defined in terms of rules with 0 or more premises and just one conclusion.

The language in which the sequents of GG are formulated is the same as the language of the impure logic of Fine (2021a) (see Section 3.1), except that each sequent is built from only *finitely* many basic formulas. Likewise, in a derivability statement $\Sigma \Vdash T$, $\Sigma$ and T are required to be finite. As they stress at the end of the paper, these restrictions can be dropped modulo minor modifications of the system and its semantics.

The rules of GG are divided into two categories, the *structural* and the *non-structural*. The structural rules are those listed in Figure 12. The non-structural rules in turn divide into two categories, the *pure* and the *impure*. Where

$$\frac{\Sigma}{\sigma}$$

is a rule with $\Sigma$ a set of sequents and $\sigma$ a sequent, let its $\Vdash$-*transform* be the rule

$$\overline{\Sigma \Vdash \sigma}$$

## The Logic of Grounding

---

$$\overline{\sigma \Vdash \sigma} \qquad \text{Identity}$$

$$\frac{\Sigma \Vdash T}{\Sigma, \Sigma' \Vdash T, T'} \qquad \text{Thinning}$$

$$\frac{\sigma, \Sigma \Vdash T \quad \Sigma' \Vdash T', \sigma}{\Sigma, \Sigma' \Vdash T, T'} \qquad \text{Snip}$$

---

**Figure 12** Structural rules for GG

GG's pure non-structural rules are the rule

$$\overline{\phi \preceq \psi \Vdash \{\phi < \psi, \psi \preceq \phi\}} \qquad \text{Irreversibility}$$

plus the $\Vdash$-transforms of all the rules of PLG (formulated in GG's language) except for the transitivity rule

$$\frac{\phi < \psi \quad \psi \preceq \chi}{\phi < \chi}$$

(The latter can be obtained from the rest of the system.) GG's impure non-structural rules include the $\Vdash$-transforms of Fine's (2012a) introduction rules (see Figure 9) and the $\Vdash$-transform of Fine's (2012a) ¬¬-elimination rule (see Figure 10). The remaining impure rules correspond to Fine's (2012a) elimination rules with disjunctive conclusions (see again Figure 10). In conformity with the approach to derivability as a relation between two sets of sequents rather than between a requirement and a set of sequents (see point (1) above), corresponding to each of these elimination rules

$$\frac{\Sigma}{T_1 \mid T_2 \mid \ldots}$$

GG contains all the rules

$$\overline{\Sigma \Vdash T}$$

where T is a selection from $\{T_1, T_2, \ldots\}$.

A statement of type $\Sigma \Vdash T$ may then be said to be *derivable* from a set of such statements iff the former can be obtained from the latter by means of the rules just laid down (which can in turn be made precise in various ways, see the characterization of derivability in PLG). We will say that a set of sequents T *follows in GG* from a set of sequents $\Sigma$ iff for some (finite) $\Sigma' \subseteq \Sigma$ and $T' \subseteq T$, $\Sigma' \Vdash T'$ is derivable from the empty set.

The basic structures invoked in the semantics are *selection systems*. A selection system is a tuple $\langle \mathcal{F}, \sqcap, \sqcup \rangle$, where $\mathcal{F}$ (conditions) is a non-empty set and $\sqcap$ (combination) and $\sqcup$ (choice) are two mappings that take finite (possibly empty) sequences of pairs of elements of $\mathcal{F}$ into elements of $\mathcal{F}$, such that $\sqcap \langle v \rangle = \sqcup \langle v \rangle$ for any pair $v$ of elements of $\mathcal{F}$.[42] Pairs of conditions in selection systems are called *contents*, and they indeed play the role of semantic values of (basic) sentences (see below).

deRosset and Fine give an informal interpretation of the operations of a selection system in terms of *menus*. Very roughly, on that interpretation, the combination operation generates conjunctive menus like a menu that would feature only 'bacon and eggs' (a strange kind of menu which offers no choice) and the choice operation generates disjunctive menus like a menu that would feature only 'bacon or eggs' (a standard kind of menu, which does offer a choice). But there is another interpretation which is fully justified by the semantic treatment of object language conjunction and disjunction (see below), and which motivated my use of the symbol $\sqcap$ for combination and of $\sqcup$ for choice (deRosset and Fine use significantly different symbols): combination and choice are at bottom mappings of conjunction and disjunction, respectively. Seen that way, selection systems are thus in some important ways similar to the structures I invoke in Correia (2023): they take a mapping of conjunction and a mapping of disjunction as sui generis mappings on semantic values of sentences. A big difference, though, is that whereas I took the mappings to be mappings from *sets* of unanalysed objects to unanalysed objects of the same sort (facts), deRosset and Fine take them to be mappings from *sequences* of *pairs* of unanalysed objects to unanalysed objects of the same sort (conditions).

Each selection system $\mathfrak{S} = \langle \mathcal{F}, \sqcap, \sqcup \rangle$ comes with a relation $\ll_\mathfrak{S}$ of *immediate selection* between sets of contents and conditions. It is defined as follows (where S is a set of contents and $F \in \mathcal{F}$):

- S $\ll_\mathfrak{S}$ F iff$_{df}$
  - either there is a sequence of contents Z such that $F = \sqcap Z$ and S and Z have the same members
  - or there is a sequence of contents Z such that $F = \sqcup Z$ and S = $\{v\}$ for some $v \in Z$

(Despite the 'either-or' phrasing, the disjunction is intended to be inclusive.) The relation $<_\mathfrak{S}$ of *strict selection* is defined as the smallest relation ▷ between

---

[42] For the sake of readability, here and below I omit the brackets (and) when mentioning applications of $\sqcap$ and $\sqcup$.

# The Logic of Grounding

sets of contents and contents that satisfies the following conditions, where $S \triangleright^* v$ iff$_{df}$ for some $F \in \mathcal{F}$, $S \triangleright \langle \sqcap \langle v \rangle, F \rangle$:

- If $S \ll_\varepsilon F$, then $S \triangleright \langle f, G \rangle$     Basis
- If $S \triangleright v$, then $S \triangleright \langle \sqcap \langle v \rangle, F \rangle$     Ascent
- If $S_1 \triangleright^* v_1, \ldots, S_n \triangleright^* v_n$ and $v_1, \ldots, v_n \triangleright v$,

  then $S_1, \ldots, S_n \triangleright v$     Lower Cut
- If $S_1 \triangleright v_1, \ldots, S_n \triangleright v_n$ and $v_1, \ldots, v_n \triangleright^* v$,

  then $S_1, \ldots, S_n \triangleright v$     Upper Cut

The corresponding starred relation, the relation of *weak selection* of the selection system, is denoted by $\leqslant_\varepsilon$. Partial notions are then defined as follows: $v \leqslant_\varepsilon w$ iff$_{df}$ for some set of contents $S$ with $v \in S$, $S \leqslant_\varepsilon w$; $v <_\varepsilon w$ iff$_{df}$ $v \leqslant_\varepsilon w$ but not $w \leqslant_\varepsilon v$.

The selection systems that are invoked to interpret the language of GG are selection systems that satisfy two further conditions[43]:

- If $S <_\varepsilon v$ iff $S \leqslant_\varepsilon v$ and for no $w \in S$ is it

  the case that $v \leqslant_\varepsilon w$     Irreversibility
- If $S <_\varepsilon \langle \sqcap \langle v_1, \ldots, v_n \rangle, F \rangle$, then for some covering $\{S_1, \ldots, S_n\}$ of $S$, $S_i \leqslant_\varepsilon v_i$ for each $i$
- If $S <_\varepsilon \langle \sqcup \langle v_1, \ldots, v_n \rangle, F \rangle$, then for some non-empty subset $\{w_1, \ldots, w_k\}$ of members of $\{v_1, \ldots, v_n\}$ and some

  covering $\{S_1, \ldots, S_k\}$ of $S$, $S_i \leqslant_\varepsilon w_i$ for each $i$     Maximality

We call them *selection frames*. A *selection model* is a selection frame endowed with an interpretation function that takes each atomic sentence into a content of the selection frame. Given a selection model $\mathfrak{M} = \langle \mathcal{F}, \sqcap, \sqcup, [\,] \rangle$, the interpretation function $[\,]$ is extended to all basic sentences of the language via the following clauses:

- $[\neg \phi] = \langle G, \sqcap \langle [\phi] \rangle \rangle$ where $[\phi] = \langle f, G \rangle$
- $[\phi \wedge \psi] = \langle \sqcap \langle [\phi], [\psi] \rangle, \sqcup \langle [\neg \phi], [\neg \psi] \rangle \rangle$
- $[\phi \vee \psi] = \langle \sqcup \langle [\phi], [\psi] \rangle, \sqcap \langle [\neg \phi], [\neg \psi] \rangle \rangle$

Where $\mathfrak{F} = \langle \mathcal{F}, \sqcap, \sqcup \rangle$, the semantic clauses for the sequents of the language are then, unsurprisingly:

- $\Delta \leqslant \phi$ holds in $\mathfrak{M}$ iff $[\Delta] \leqslant_\mathfrak{F} [\phi]$
- $\phi \preccurlyeq \psi$ holds in $\mathfrak{M}$ iff $[\phi] \leqslant_\mathfrak{F} [\psi]$
- $\Delta < \phi$ holds in $\mathfrak{M}$ iff $[\Delta] <_\mathfrak{F} [\phi]$
- $\phi < \psi$ holds in $\mathfrak{M}$ iff $[\phi] <_\mathfrak{F} [\psi]$

---

[43] The notion of covering is defined in footnote 24.

A set of sequents T is said to be a *GG-consequence* of a set of sequents Σ iff for every model 𝔐 in which all the members of Σ hold, some member of T holds in 𝔐.

deRosset and Fine establish that GG is sound and complete with respect to the proposed semantics:

**Theorem 13** (Soundness and completeness for GG). *For all sets of sequents Σ and T, T follows in GG from Σ iff T is a GG-consequence of Σ.*

deRosset and Fine's logic of grounding is subject to an objection somewhat akin to the second objection against ILFG mentioned at the end of Section 3.5. The immediate selection relation $\ll_\mathfrak{S}$ of a selection system $\mathfrak{S}$ only takes as 'right-hand side' relata items that are combinations or choices. As a consequence, a strict full grounding sequent $\Delta < \phi$ holds in a selection model only if in that model, $\phi$ expresses a content of type $\langle F, G \rangle$ where $F$ is a combination or a choice. Now consider a 'real life' sentence of strict full grounding such as 'the fact that Socrates exists metaphysically grounds the fact that {Socrates} exists', and assume it is true. Suppose we want to build a selection model in which the sentence, understood as a sequent of type $\phi < \psi$, holds. Then by the previous remark, we will have to treat the sentence '{Socrates} exists' as expressing a content whose first element is a combination or a choice. But a combination or a choice *of what*? If the sentence were conjunctive or disjunctive, for instance, then there would be a natural answer. But the sentence does not have any logical complexity (or so am I assuming for the sake of the argument), and therefore, it would seem, the only models that we can come up with will be artificial models, models that do not faithfully represent the real content of the sentence. The objection, stated in a nutshell, is that the proposed semantics cannot be applied in a non-artificial way to *all* sentences that express links of strict full metaphysical grounding.

## 3.7 Further Works

Other studies on the logic of grounding would deserve to be duly presented, but for lack of space I offer here only a brief survey. I would classify all the studies mentioned below as representational (in the sense introduced on page 47). With the exception of Poggiolesi's (2016, 2018) work, they all target a notion of strict full grounding that obey the Finean introduction rules (see Figure 9) or a partial notion that obeys the rules for partial strict grounding (i.e., the relation Fine symbolizes by $<^*$, see page 8) that can be derived from them.

Batchelor (2010) and Schnieder (2011) are two very early works on the logic of grounding. Batchelor starts with a theory of a relation $I$ of immediate partial grounding and defines a relation $G$ of partial grounding as the ancestral of $I$.

He then takes a fact $F$ to be strictly fully grounded in some facts iff (i) the latter facts are all partial grounds, in the sense of $G$, of $F$ and (ii) they together necessarily imply $F$. Schnieder focuses exclusively on partial strict grounding. He gives an axiomatic proof system for the notion and establishes its consistency.

Korbmacher (2018a, 2018b) also focuses exclusively on partial strict grounding. In Korbmacher (2018a), he introduces and develops an axiomatic theory of (type-free) truth and partial strict grounding based on an axiomatic theory of Peano arithmetic, in the spirit of the axiomatic theories of truth discussed in Halbach (2011). In Korbmacher (2018b), he studies an extension of the previous theory with a Tarski-style hierarchy of typed truth predicates.

In Correia (2014), I offer a tree-theoretic characterization of *logical* grounding and use that notion (i) to characterize well-known consequence relations, among them classical consequence and the consequence relation corresponding to Anderson and Belnap's (1962, 1963) first-degree entailments (FDEs), and (ii) to formulate a ground-theoretic version of (part of) Kripke's (1975) celebrated theory of truth. In Correia (2015), I develop further the study of the connections between logical grounding and FDEs: I axiomatize the logic of FDEs understood as multiple-conclusion sequents and then show that various notions of logical grounding can be axiomatized by modifying in very simple ways the system for FDEs.

Poggiolesi, (2016, 2018) also focuses on logical grounding, but her target notion is a peculiar notion of logical grounding she dubs 'complete immediate grounding'. The notion can be grasped by means of a couple of examples: the complete immediate ground of a conjunctive truth $\phi \wedge \psi$ is the plurality of truths $\phi, \psi$; by contrast, the complete immediate ground of a disjunctive truth $\phi \vee \psi$ is not always the same – it is $\phi$ if $\psi$ is false, $\psi$ if $\phi$ is false, and the plurality $\phi, \psi$ if none is false. In order to take this sort of variability into account, Poggiolesi takes complete immediate grounding to be a *ternary* relation linking a groundee, its complete immediate ground and an extra relatum intended to specify under which condition the link of complete immediate grounding holds. More precisely, her basic notion is that of a multiset of formulas $\Delta$ grounding a formula $\phi$ under the condition that a formula $\psi$ holds.

Krämer's (2018) starting point is Fine's truthmaker semantics, but he enriches the conceptual framework with the idea of *modes of verification*: the new idea is that of a verifier verifying a proposition *by verifying* other propositions. Disjunctive propositions provide straightforward illustrations of this idea: any verifier of $P(Q)$ verifies $P \vee Q$ by verifying $P(Q)$. Krämer actually works with two types of propositions, 'unilateral' propositions and 'bilateral' propositions. Krämer identifies unilateral propositions with sets of modes of verification, and bilateral propositions with pairs of such sets, where the first member of such a pair (its 'positive' component) corresponds to the ways of verifying the proposition and the second member (its 'negative' component) to the ways of falsifying it. He accordingly introduces two types of grounding relations, those which relate unilateral propositions and those which relate bilateral propositions. On his account, unilateral propositions $P_1, \ldots, P_n$ strictly ground unilateral proposition $P$ just in case (i) there is such a thing as the mode of verifying 'by verifying $P_1, \ldots, P_n$' and (ii) this mode is a member of $P$. Grounding between bilateral propositions is simply defined by 'focusing on positive components': for instance, Krämer takes $\langle P_1, Q_1 \rangle, \ldots, \langle P_n, Q_n \rangle$ to strictly ground $\langle P, Q \rangle$ just in case $P_1, \ldots, P_n$ strictly ground $P$.

In Correia (2021b), I present a logic (semantics + adequate proof system) for relative fundamentality – more precisely, for the notion of *being more fundamental than, or as fundamental as* – as well as a modal extension of that logic. I then suggest a definition of strict full grounding in terms of necessity and relative fundamentality, and I investigate the logical properties of the notion given this definition and the underlying modal logic of relative fundamentality.

## 4 Further Topics

In this last section, I would like to elaborate a bit on two important topics within the formal theory of grounding. The first topic, discussed in Section 4.1, has been touched upon in previous parts of this work. The second topic, discussed in Section 4.2, has not yet been addressed at all.

### 4.1 Ground-Theoretic Equivalence, Metaphysical Equivalence and Identity

In this section, I will assume that grounding statements express, at the semantic level, relations between certain entities. This is of course a natural view to have if one takes grounding statements to involve *predicates* for the corresponding notions of grounding, but one may also hold that view while taking grounding statements to involve *operators* rather than predicates for the corresponding notions. In fact, even though the approaches to the logic of grounding presented in Sections 3.1 to 3.6 have it that the linguistic expressions for grounding are sentential operators rather than predicates, they all treat grounding statements as corresponding, at the semantic level, to relations between certain entities. I called these entities 'facts' or 'propositions', depending on the particular view at stake. For the sake of neutrality, I will here use the label 'g-contents' instead.[44]

---

[44] This section heavily draws on Correia (2020). As I argue there, taking grounding statements to express relations is not strictly speaking required to go through the discussion below: one could make do with higher-order quantification and other higher-order resources instead.

Three equivalence relations between g-contents have been of particular importance in studies about grounding: *ground-theoretic equivalence, metaphysical equivalence* and *identity*. The latter relation is plain numerical identity. The other two relations can be defined as follows, where < is here used as a *predicate* for non-factive strict full grounding understood as a relation between g-contents:

- $x$ is ground-theoretically equivalent to $y$ iff$_{df}$ (i) whatever grounds one grounds the other and (ii) whatever one helps to ground, the other also grounds in the same way – with symbols: (i) for all pluralities of g-contents $Z$, $Z < x$ iff $Z < y$ and (ii) for all pluralities of g-contents $Z$ and all g-contents $z$, $Z,x < z$ iff $Z,y < z$.
- $x$ is metaphysically equivalent to $y$ iff$_{df}$ to say that $x$ holds and to say that $y$ holds is to describe the world as being the same way.[45]

Once equipped with the notions of ground-theoretic equivalence and metaphysical equivalence as they have just been defined, one can define corresponding relations for *sentences* of some language or languages, by saying that two sentences are ground-theoretically equivalent (metaphysically equivalent) just in case the g-contents they express are ground-theoretically equivalent (metaphysically equivalent). Depending on the context, it may be relevant to directly invoke these sentential notions rather than their content-theoretic counterparts, and vice versa.

### 4.1.1 Two Applications: The Granularity Question and the Worldly / Representational Distinction

The previous point is illustrated by the formulation of the 'granularity question' for grounding and the characterization of the worldly / representational distinction. The granularity question for grounding is the question of 'how fine-grained grounding is'. A very natural precisification of the question invokes sentential ground-theoretic equivalence:

- Which sentences (of a given language or of given languages) are ground-theoretically equivalent?[46]

In Section 3.5, I introduced the worldly / representational distinction by saying that a notion of grounding is worldly if it is sensitive only to how the world is, and that it is representational otherwise. A more precise characterization

---

[45] I propose this definition in Correia (2020) (footnote 16).
[46] I propose this precisification in Correia (2020).

of being worldly goes as follows, where only content-theoretic notions are invoked:

- A notion of grounding is worldly iff any two g-contents are ground-theoretically equivalent (where ground-theoretic equivalence is defined in term of the notion of grounding in question) if they are metaphysically equivalent.[47]

A direct consequence of this characterization is that for any notion of grounding, if metaphysical equivalence between g-contents entails identity, then that notion of grounding is worldly.

### 4.1.2 Relations between the Three Notions

What are the relations between ground-theoretic equivalence, metaphysical equivalence and identity? By Leibniz's Law, of course, g-content identity entails both ground-theoretic and metaphysical equivalence. But are there other entailments between the three relations, and if so, which ones? Various theories give various answers to the question. Let me run through some of them.

As we saw, the logics put forward in Correia (2010, 2017) contain an explicit logic of factual / propositional equivalence – symbolized in both papers by $\approx$ – and semantically, factual / propositional equivalence is interpreted as g-content identity. In Correia (2010), I stipulate that factual equivalence stands for metaphysical equivalence understood as defined above. Therefore, on the view I explore there, metaphysical equivalence entails identity. (From which it follows that the notion targeted by the view is worldly – see two paragraphs back.) Not so on the view explored in Correia (2017), at least given some assumptions about what is metaphysically equivalent to what that I find plausible. Given any $\phi$, the 2017 logic takes the contents of $\phi$, $\phi \wedge \phi$, $\phi \vee \phi$ and $\neg\neg\phi$ to be pairwise distinct. Yet I am very much inclined to take $\phi$, $\phi \wedge \phi$, $\phi \vee \phi$ and $\neg\neg\phi$ to be metaphysically equivalent, for any $\phi$.

Does ground-theoretic equivalence entail identity on these views? Correia (2017) contains a *proof* that this is the case in the logic it puts forward. I do not know whether the entailment holds in the logic explored in Correia (2010).

An upshot of the previous considerations is that metaphysical equivalence entails ground-theoretic equivalence in the logic of Correia (2010) but not in the logic of Correia (2017). Another upshot is that the converse entailment

---

[47] In the main text of Correia (2020), I formulate essentially the same characterization but with a linguistic flavour, using a *sentential* notion of metaphysical equivalence which I call there 'descriptive equivalence'. The non-linguistic formulation that I mention here is suggested in footnote 16 of the same paper.

holds in the logic of Correia (2017), and that I do not know whether it holds in the logic of Correia (2010).

In Correia (2016), I present a proof system for the logic of factual equivalence, which, as in Correia (2010), I understand as standing for metaphysical equivalence. I provide two alternative semantic characterizations of the system. One of them is within Fine's truthmaker framework, and it deems a sentence of type $\phi \approx \psi$ true when $\phi$ and $\psi$ have the same 'positive content' in Fine's (2012a) sense, that is, when the set of verifiers of $\phi$ = the set of verifiers of $\psi$ (see Section 3.1). If we assume, in line with Fine (2012a) and Fine (2012b), that a g-content is a set of states closed under fusion, then the view put forward in Correia (2016) naturally extends to a view according to which two g-contents are metaphysically equivalent only if they are identical. On such a view, of course, metaphysical equivalence entails ground-theoretic equivalence.[48]

Correia (2016) does not offer a specific account of grounding, but it presupposes that the kind of account put forward in Correia (2010) and Fine (2012a, 2012b) is correct. I have a proof, too long to include here, that on Fine's truthmaker version of the account, ground-theoretic equivalence between g-contents entails identity (and hence metaphysical equivalence). The proof assumes that a state has a proper part only if it admits of a decomposition into proper parts. The assumption is not built into the truthmaker framework, but is it a rather natural assumption to make.

As we saw (Section 3.7), Krämer (2018) features two relations of strict full grounding, one relating unilateral propositions and the other one relating bilateral propositions. Each gives rise to its own notion of ground-theoretic equivalence. Let us first focus on the unilateral notion.

It can be shown that ground-theoretic equivalence between unilateral propositions entails identity.[49] Krämer does not discuss metaphysical equivalence, but its connections with identity and ground-theoretic equivalence in his framework can nevertheless be identified, in part with the help of extra assumptions. Given that ground-theoretic equivalence between unilateral propositions entails identity, it ipso facto entail metaphysical equivalence. I find it utterly plausible that $\phi$ and $\phi \wedge \phi$ are metaphysically equivalent for any $\phi$. On Krämer's account, $\phi$ and $\phi \wedge \phi$ always express distinct unilateral propositions. Hence,

---

[48] Correia (2023) introduces two logics for factual equivalence which in their own ways generalize the logic in Correia (2016): in both logics, a notion of logical *consequence* is characterized, both proof-theoretically and semantically, and one of the two logics allows for the formation of conjunctions and disjunctions of arbitrary lengths. The semantics is formulated in the framework described in Section 3.4, and it also interprets $\phi \approx \psi$ as expressing g-content identity.

[49] This follows from Lemma 2.1 and Lemma 3.1 in the appendix of Krämer (2018) (assuming that strict full grounding is irreflexive). In Correia, (2020), I mistakenly claim that on Krämer's account, ground-theoretic equivalence between *bilateral* propositions entails identity.

assuming I am right about self-conjunctions, on his account, metaphysical equivalence between unilateral propositions does not entail identity. It follows that metaphysical equivalence between unilateral propositions does not entail ground-theoretic equivalence.

Let us move on to the bilateral case. Krämer establishes that bilateral propositions $\langle P, P' \rangle$ and $\langle Q, Q' \rangle$ are ground-theoretically equivalent iff $P = Q$. It immediately follows that ground-theoretic equivalence between bilateral propositions does not entail identity. Self-conjunctions can again be used to show that bilateral propositions may be metaphysically equivalent without being identical. On Krämer's account, if $\phi$ expresses the bilateral proposition $\langle P, Q \rangle$, then $\phi \wedge \phi$ expresses a bilateral proposition $\langle f(P), g(Q) \rangle$ where $f(P) \neq P$ (it is not important for my purposes to specify exactly the nature of functions $f$ and $g$). Granted that $\phi$ and $\phi \wedge \phi$ are metaphysically equivalent, it follows that on Krämer's account, metaphysical equivalence between bilateral propositions does not entail identity. It also follows, via the result established by Krämer mentioned above, that metaphysical equivalence between bilateral propositions does not entail ground-theoretic equivalence. Does ground-theoretic equivalence between bilateral propositions entail metaphysical equivalence? Krämer's account of ground-theoretic equivalence alone does not decide the question.

### 4.1.3 Interaction with Conjunction, Disjunction and Negation

Let me finally turn to the question of how ground-theoretic equivalence, metaphysical equivalence and g-content identity interact with conjunction, disjunction and negation. There are actually *two* questions here, depending on whether conjunction, disjunction and negation are understood as *operations on g-contents* or as *sentential operators*. Let me call the first question *content-theoretic* and the second question *linguistic*. A theory which addresses the content-theoretic question for, say, ground-theoretic equivalence will decide whether claims such as the following ones are true, where ⊓ is an operation of g-content-conjunction and − an operation of g-content-negation:

- $X \sqcap Y$ is ground-theoretically equivalent to $Y \sqcap X$
- $--X$ is ground-theoretically equivalent to $X$
- If $X$ is ground-theoretically equivalent to $Y$, then so is $-X$ to $-Y$

By contrast, a theory which addresses the linguistic question for ground-theoretic equivalence will take as given a mapping [ ] from sentences of some language to g-contents, and will decide whether claims such as the following ones are true, where ∧ is a conjunction operator and ¬ a negation operator:

- [ϕ ∧ ψ] is ground-theoretically equivalent to [ψ ∧ ϕ]
- [¬¬ϕ] is ground-theoretically equivalent to [ϕ]
- If [ϕ] is ground-theoretically equivalent to [ψ], then so is [¬ϕ] to [¬ψ]

All the theories of g-content that have been discussed so far feature an operation of conjunction and an operation of disjunction on g-contents. Some also feature an operation of negation, but some do not. Since these theories are nevertheless all coupled with a semantics for (linguistic) conjunction, disjunction *and* negation, let me put aside the content-theoretic question and focus on the linguistic question instead.

As before, let us suppose given a pool of atomic sentences and define the basic sentences relative to that pool as the sentences that can be built from the atomic sentences using ∧, ∨, ¬ and the brackets (and). For the purpose of theorizing about ground-theoretic equivalence, metaphysical equivalence and g-content identity, we may introduce the sentential operators $\approx_{GT}$, $\approx_M$ and $\approx_I$, respectively, together with the following intended intuitive semantics:

- $\phi \approx_{GT} \psi$ is true iff $\phi$'s g-content is ground-theoretically equivalent to $\psi$'s g-content
- $\phi \approx_M \psi$ is true iff $\phi$'s g-content is metaphysically equivalent to $\psi$'s g-content
- $\phi \approx_I \psi$ is true iff $\phi$'s g-content = $\psi$'s g-content

(As far as the discussion to come is concerned, we could take the three symbols to be predicates of sentences rather than sentential operators.)

As we saw, Correia (2010) puts forward a logic for $\approx_M$, which also counts as a logic for $\approx_I$, and Correia (2017) puts forward a logic for $\approx_I$, which also counts as a logic for $\approx_{GT}$. In these logics, equivalence sentences can be parts of more complex sentences. Let us here focus on languages that only have equivalence sentences, and address the question of which such sentences are true in virtue of their logical form. And let me use the symbol ≈ without specifying which notion it is supposed to express.

In Correia (2020), following Krämer (2021), I discuss five relevant systems. I reproduce some of the discussion here, and make connections with previous parts of this Element. The five systems are the Hilbert-style systems defined in Figures 13 to 17 (the labels are from Correia 2020).

**C$_{2017}$** is a system which captures the logically true formulas of type $\phi \approx \psi$ that one gets on the basis of the logic discussed in Correia (2017). As we saw, in that logic ≈ expresses g-content identity, and can also be understood as expressing ground-theoretic equivalence. **K$_{int}$** and **K$_{ext}$** are the 'intermediate' system

*Axioms*

A1. $\phi \wedge \psi \approx \psi \wedge \phi$
A2. $\phi \vee \psi \approx \psi \vee \phi$
A3. $\phi \approx \phi$

*Rules*

R1. $\phi \approx \psi \:/\: \psi \approx \phi$
R2. $\phi \approx \psi, \psi \approx \chi \:/\: \phi \approx \chi$
R3. $\phi \approx \psi \:/\: \phi \wedge \chi \approx \psi \wedge \chi$
R4. $\phi \approx \psi \:/\: \phi \vee \chi \approx \psi \vee \chi$
R5. $\phi \approx \psi \:/\: \neg \phi \approx \neg \psi$

**Figure 13** System $\mathbf{C_{2017}}$

*Axioms*

Like $\mathbf{C_{2017}}$, plus:

A4. $\neg(\phi \wedge \psi) \approx \neg\phi \vee \neg\psi$
A5. $\neg(\phi \vee \psi) \approx \neg\phi \wedge \neg\psi$

*Rules*

Like $\mathbf{C_{2017}}$, minus R5, plus:

R6. $\phi \approx \psi \:/\: \neg\neg\phi \approx \neg\neg\psi$

**Figure 14** System $\mathbf{K_{int}}$

*Axioms*

Like $\mathbf{K_{int}}$, plus:

A6. $\phi \wedge \phi \approx \phi \vee \phi$
A7. $\phi \vee \phi \approx \neg\neg\phi$

*Rules*

Like $\mathbf{K_{int}}$, plus:

R7. $\phi \in \psi, \phi \in \chi \:/\: \phi \in (\psi \wedge \chi)$
R8. $\phi \in \psi \:/\: \phi \in (\psi \vee \chi)$

where $\phi \in \psi$ is used for $\phi \vee \psi \approx \psi \vee \psi$

**Figure 15** System $\mathbf{K_{ext}}$

*Axioms*

Like $\mathbf{K_{int}}$, minus A3, plus:

A8. $\phi \approx \neg\neg\phi$
A9. $\phi \approx \phi \wedge \phi$
A10. $\phi \approx \phi \vee \phi$
A11. $\phi \wedge (\psi \wedge \chi) \approx (\phi \wedge \psi) \wedge \chi$
A12. $\phi \vee (\psi \vee \chi) \approx (\phi \vee \psi) \vee \chi$
A13. $\phi \wedge (\psi \vee \chi) \approx (\phi \wedge \psi) \vee (\phi \wedge \chi)$

*Rules*

Like $\mathbf{K_{int}}$, minus R6

**Figure 16** System $\mathbf{C_{2016}}$

*Axioms*

Like $\mathbf{C_{2016}}$, plus:

A14. $\phi \vee (\psi \wedge \chi) \approx (\phi \vee \psi) \wedge (\phi \vee \chi)$

*Rules*

Like $\mathbf{C_{2016}}$

**Figure 17** System $\mathbf{C_{2010}}$

and the 'extensional' system, respectively, of Krämer (2021). Krämer interprets $\approx$ in both systems as expressing ground-theoretic equivalence between bilateral propositions, as they are defined in his 2018 paper. $\mathbf{C_{2016}}$ is the system for metaphysical equivalence discussed in Correia (2016). As we saw, given certain assumptions, $\approx$ as semantically characterized there can also be understood as expressing both g-content identity and ground-theoretic equivalence. Finally, $\mathbf{C_{2010}}$ has the same theorems as R. B. Angell's (1989) system for 'analytic equivalence' (see Fine 2016 for the axiomatization presented here), and it is a system which captures the logically true formulas of type $\phi \approx \psi$ that one gets on the basis of the system discussed in Correia (2010). As we saw, in that system $\approx$ is interpreted as metaphysical equivalence and is semantically interpreted as expressing g-content identity. These systems are related as follows, where $\longrightarrow$ represents strict inclusion between systems ($S_1 \longrightarrow S_2$ means that all theorems of $S_1$ are theorems of $S_2$ but not vice versa)[50]:

$$\mathbf{C_{2017}} \longrightarrow \mathbf{K_{int}} \longrightarrow \mathbf{K_{ext}} \longrightarrow \mathbf{C_{2016}} \longrightarrow \mathbf{C_{2010}}$$

---

[50] The corresponding diagram in Correia (2020) is incorrect: I overlooked the fact that $\mathbf{K_{ext}}$ is included in $\mathbf{C_{2016}}$ (which can be easily established given Lemma 3.5 of Correia 2016 and basic facts about $\mathbf{C_{2016}}$). Thanks to Shogo Tsuboi for bringing this point to my attention.

In the proposed axiomatizations, the axioms and rules of $C_{2016}$ are exactly those of $C_{2010}$, *minus the distributivity axiom A14*. What justification can be given for not having A14 as an axiom?

We saw in Section 3.3 that $\phi \vee (\psi \wedge \chi)$ and $(\phi \vee \psi) \wedge (\phi \vee \chi)$ need not have the same verifiers. If we take seriously the view that metaphysical equivalence corresponds semantically to sameness of g-content, and if we take the g-content associated with a sentence to be the set of its verifiers, then we have a justification for not taking A14 as axiomatic if $\approx$ represents metaphysical equivalence.

There is another justification (or perhaps better: motivation) that I advertised at the beginning of Section 3.4: A14 conflicts with some intuitions about grounding. More precisely, A14, understood with $\approx$ expressing metaphysical equivalence, conflicts with grounding understood as worldly. For assume $\phi < \phi \vee \neg\psi$ and $\psi < \phi \vee \psi$, where $<$ stands for worldly strict full grounding (factive or non-factive, it does not matter). As an illustration, we may take $\phi = $ 'Snow is white' and $\psi = $ 'Socrates is human'. From these two assumptions, one can plausibly infer $\phi, \psi < (\phi \vee \neg\psi) \wedge (\phi \vee \psi)$. It actually turns out that *all* the impure logics featuring $<$ that we previously discussed validate the inference from $\phi_1 < \psi_1$ and $\phi_2 < \psi_2$ to $\phi_1, \phi_2 < (\psi_1 \wedge \psi_2)$. Suppose now for reductio that A14 holds, where $\approx$ expresses metaphysical equivalence. Since $<$ is worldly, one can infer $\phi, \psi < \phi \vee (\neg\psi \wedge \psi)$. But intuitively, $\psi$ plays no role in fully grounding $\phi \vee (\neg\psi \wedge \psi)$. For more details, see Correia (2016) and Krämer and Roski (2015).[51]

## 4.2 Puzzles

It has been argued, first by Fine (2010) in the very early days of the contemporary research on grounding, that several sets of ground-theoretic principles which have some plausibility are nevertheless inconsistent – on their own or in conjunction with other, non-ground-theoretic principles that are themselves plausible. In this section, I discuss the Finean puzzles and some other ground-theoretic puzzles that have been recently discussed in the literature.

### 4.2.1 Fine-Style Puzzles

Fine (2010) puts forward a series of similar sets of ground-theoretic principles whose members are all plausible but which are inconsistent given a background of classical logical principles. Krämer (2013) formulates a particularly simple

---

[51] In reply to Wilhelm (2021), Litland (2021) sketches two interesting theories of propositional identity that I do not have the space to discuss here. See footnote 65 for some remarks on how propositional identity behaves on these two views.

version of the Fine-style puzzles, which has the effect of narrowing down the reasonable options for solving the other puzzles.[52]

Fine's puzzles as well as Krämer's invoke the concept of *partial strict grounding*, where a partial strict ground is a part of a strict full ground. In Section 2.1, following Fine (2012a), I used the operator $<^*$ for that notion, but here I will use $<$ instead, thereby following Fine (2010) and Krämer (2013). Both Fine and Krämer assume that partial strict grounding is factive, but the puzzles arise, actually in a more straightforward way, if the notion is assumed to be non-factive.

Here is one of Fine's argument that leads to inconsistency, almost verbatim:

(1) Something exists – in symbols: $\exists x Ex$.

(2) Therefore, the fact that something exists exists – in symbols: $E[\exists x Ex]$.

(3) Given (2), $E[\exists x Ex] < \exists x Ex$.

(4) Given (2), $\exists x Ex < E[\exists x Ex]$.

(5) $<$ is asymmetric.

(6) (3)–(5) are inconsistent.

The starting point of the argument, (1), is hard to reject. The justification of steps (2)–(4) relies on the following general principles (Fine has slightly different formulations of the principles, but the differences are immaterial for our discussion)[53]:

*Factual Existence:* If $\phi$, then $E[\phi]$;
*Existential Grounding:* If $Fa$, then $Fa < \exists x Fx$;
*Factual Grounding:* If $E[\phi]$, then $\phi < E[\phi]$.

Factual Existence justifies (2), Existential Grounding justifies (3), and Factual Grounding justifies (4). Instead of invoking the asymmetry of $<$, Fine invokes its transitivity and irreflexivity. But since asymmetry is weaker than

---

[52] For further versions of the Finean puzzles, see Correia (2011) and Donaldson (2017).
[53] In particular, he is cautious enough to formulate Existential Grounding with an existence condition in the antecedent, in order to escape objections akin to the standard objections against the classical $\exists$-introduction rule that motivate the adoption of a free logic. Note that there are similar objections against Higher-Order Existential Grounding (see below), on which Krämer's argument relies. Had Krämer been cautious enough, he would also have added an existence condition in the antecedent of the principle – something like $\exists q(\psi \doteq q)$ where $\doteq$ is akin to standard identity but of the appropriate grammatical type. And he would accordingly have needed to add a higher-order version of Fine's Factual Existence. I decided to omit these existence conditions in order to simplify a bit the discussion, but the discussion would be essentially the same if the existence conditions were added to the principles.

the combination of transitivity and irreflexivity, one gets a more compelling argument if one invokes, as I did here, the former rather than the latter.

The other puzzling arguments that Fine presents also involve the assumption that < is transitive and irreflexive – but which could, as with the previous argument, be replaced by the assumption that < is asymmetric. They concern either facts, like the previous argument, or propositions or sentences. And – crucially – they all involve either Existential Grounding or a corresponding principles for universal quantification[54]:

*Universal Grounding:* If $\forall xFx$, then $Fa < \forall xFx$.

Importantly, contrary to Factual Grounding and other ground-theoretic principles used in Fine's arguments, Existential Grounding and Universal Grounding do not feature expressions for facts, propositions or sentences.

Krämer's puzzle is very similar to the Finean puzzle introduced above. It is based on the following principle, akin to Existential Grounding but involving quantification into sentential rather than nominal position[55]:

*Higher-Order Existential Grounding:* If $\phi[\psi/p]$, then $\phi[\psi/p] < \exists p\phi$,

where $p$ is the only free variable in $\phi$, $\psi$ has no free variable, and $\phi[\psi/p]$ is the result of replacing each free occurrence of $p$ in $\phi$ by $\psi$. The argument leading to inconsistency is very short:

(1) Something is the case – in symbols: $\exists pp$.

(2) Given (1), $\exists pp < \exists pp$.

(3) < is irreflexive.

(4) (1)–(3) are inconsistent.

Step (2) is justified by Higher-Order Existential Grounding: take $p$ for $\phi$ and $\exists pp$ for $\psi$. Note that condition (3) could have been replaced by the stronger condition that < is asymmetric.

Putting aside misgivings about higher-order quantification or Modus Ponens, the options for escaping Krämer's puzzle are (i) to reject Higher-Order Existential Grounding and (ii) to reject the view that < is irreflexive. The corresponding options to escape Fine's puzzle are (a) to reject Existential Grounding and

---

[54] As with Existential Grounding, Fine adds an existence condition in the antecedent of the principle. Omitting it does not affect the discussion.

[55] Krämer actually phrases his principle in a slightly different way. I borrow (and modify a bit) Fritz's (2020) formulation here.

(b) to reject the view that $<$ is asymmetric. Of course, Fine's puzzle involves extra principles, namely Factual Existence and Factual Grounding, but if there is a solution of Krämer's puzzle along the lines of (i) or (ii), then presumably there should *at least* be a solution to Fine's puzzle along the lines of (a) or (b).[56] This can generalized to each of the Finean puzzles, replacing 'Existential Grounding' by 'Universal Grounding' if needed, according to the principle at work in the puzzle.

In light of the previous sections, what are the options on the table? Most of the logics discussed in Section 3 validate the following principle for $<$[57]:

*Disjunctive Grounding:* If $\phi$, then $\phi < \phi \vee \psi$;
If $\psi$, then $\psi < \phi \vee \psi$.

Among the logics which countenance Disjunctive Grounding and which also deal with the interaction between grounding and the quantifiers, most also countenance Existential Grounding. This is not surprising: given the similarities between existential quantification and disjunction, it is indeed hard to see how one could accept Disjunctive Grounding and reject Existential Grounding. Even if it is not *formally* impossible to do it (see for instance Fine 2010, §7), it is not clear – to me at least! – that going that way is philosophically satisfactory. For the logics under consideration, rejecting the asymmetry of $<$ as a way out of the Finean puzzle presented above strikes me as the best way to go – and I have the same opinion about the other Finean puzzles, on similar grounds.[58] Likewise, I take it that for these logics, rejecting the irreflexivity of $<$ is the best way to go in reaction to Krämer's puzzle.[59]

The logics discussed in Section 3 that *do not* validate Disjunctive Grounding are the logics of worldly grounding of Fine (2012a) (semantic side), Correia (2010), Lovett (2020a) and Correia (2023) (see Sections 3.1–3.4). (It is easy to see why they reject Disjunctive Grounding: they reject the possibility that $\phi < \phi \vee \phi$.) Given that they reject Disjunctive Grounding, it is natural to suspect that they also reject Existential Grounding, or that they would reject it once

---

[56] I say 'at least' because a view that rules out Existential Grounding or the asymmetry of $<$ may also rule out Factual Existence or Factual Grounding. See footnote 61 for an illustration.
[57] Remember that here $<$ stands for partial strict grounding understood factively. When I say that a logic validates this principle, I mean that it either validates a formal implementation of the principle, or would do it if the relevant object language had an operator for $<$ and relevant systematic / semantic adjustments were made.
[58] I advocate, in effect, this option in Correia (2014) when discussing a case of mutual grounding that arises from a version of Existential Grounding for a non-factive notion of strict full grounding.
[59] Woods (2018) advocates this option in reaction to the puzzle.

suitably extended to take care of quantified statements if this is not already the case. I think the suspicion is correct.[60]

As we saw, in these logics, factive strict full grounding is definable in terms of a non-factive notion of weak full grounding – or, equivalently, a notion of disjunctive parthood – in the very same way. Indeed – focusing on definability in terms of weak full grounding for the sake of illustration – these logics all agree on the following biconditional:

(Def) Some facts $F_1, F_2, \ldots$ factively strictly fully ground a fact $G$ iff (i) $F_1$, $F_2, \ldots$ all obtain, (ii) $F_1, F_2, \ldots$ non-factively weakly fully ground $G$, and (iii) $G$ does not help non-factively weakly fully ground any of the $F_i$s.

All the logics in question also validate the following principle, akin to Disjunctive Grounding (but without the conditional form since $\leqslant$ is non-factive):

*Weak Disjunctive Grounding:* $\phi \leqslant \phi \vee \psi$;
$\psi \leqslant \phi \vee \psi$.

Given (Def), and given that a partial strict ground is a part of a strict full ground, the logics validate the following restricted version of Disjunctive Grounding, where $\preccurlyeq$ is the partial notion corresponding to $\leqslant$:

*Restricted Disjunctive Grounding:* If $\phi$ and $\phi \vee \psi \not\leqslant \phi$, then $\phi \prec \phi \vee \psi$;
If $\psi$ and $\phi \vee \psi \not\leqslant \psi$, then $\psi \prec \phi \vee \psi$.

Turning now to the quantifiers, given that Weak Disjunctive Grounding is accepted, so should presumably be its existential counterpart:

*Weak Existential Grounding:* $Fa \leqslant \exists x Fx$.

From this and (Def) we then only get a restricted version of Existential Grounding:

*Restricted Existential Grounding:* If $Fa$ and $\exists x Fx \not\leqslant Fa$, then $Fa \prec \exists x Fx$.

There is no way, in the spirit of the logics under consideration, to get the unrestricted version.

With Restricted Existential Grounding rather than Existential Grounding in place, the Finean argument does not go through. At line (3), instead of getting $E[\exists x Ex] \prec \exists x Ex$ tout court, we get it *conditional on the truth of* $\exists x Ex \not\leqslant E[\exists x Ex]$. The latter is not guaranteed to be true – even worse, what

---

[60] See Lovett (2020b) for considerations similar to those that follow.

we arrived at line (4), namely $\exists xEx < E[\exists xEx]$, entails that $\exists xEx \not\preccurlyeq E[\exists xEx]$ is *false*! Thus, we cannot infer $E[\exists xEx] < \exists xEx$ and so we cannot conclude to inconsistency via the asymmetry of $<$.[61]

Similar considerations hold for the other Finean puzzles – I leave the details aside. Similar considerations also hold for Krämer's puzzle, but since the details are very few in number let me go through them. In the spirit of the logics under consideration, Higher-Order Existential Grounding should be replaced by the appropriate restriction:

*Restricted Higher-Order Existential Grounding:* If $\phi[\psi/p]$ and $\exists p\phi \not\preccurlyeq \phi[\psi/p]$, then $\phi[\psi/p] < \exists p\phi$.

Instantiate in the same way as before and you get: if $\exists pp$ and $\exists pp \not\preccurlyeq \exists pp$, then $\exists pp < \exists pp$. Now the second condition is false since $\preccurlyeq$ is reflexive. Puzzle solved.

The previous discussion of the Fine-style puzzles would deserve more space; the interested reader may consult Krämer (2020) for a very good complement. Before leaving this topic, though, let me briefly comment upon Fritz (2020), which elaborates on Krämer's puzzle in an interesting way (and which Krämer 2020 does not discuss).

Fritz explores the idea of rejecting Higher-Order Existential Grounding while at the same time accepting another higher-order principle that expresses the same core idea. This other principle, $(\exists Q)$, is formulated in a language that allows for both quantification into sentential position and quantification into sentential operator position:

$(\exists Q)$ $\forall X \forall p(Xp \supset (Xp < EX))$.

In $(\exists Q)$, $p$ is (as before) a sentential variable, $X$ is a monadic sentential operator variable, and $EX$ is the Frege-friendly way of expressing what in the more standard notation we would express by means of a formula like $\exists qXq$. (Frege held the view that quantifiers are properties of properties.) Instantiate $X$ with a given operator $T$ and $p$ with $ET$ and you get:

$(\exists Q^+)$ $T(ET) \supset (T(ET) < ET)$.

---

[61] Interestingly, friends of the logics under consideration also have a good reason to reject the combination of Factual Existence and Factual Grounding. Given the truism $\exists xEx$, from these two principles one can indeed infer $\exists xEx < E[\exists xEx]$. The latter entails $E[\exists xEx] \not\preccurlyeq \exists xEx$, which entails $E[\exists xEx] \not\leqslant \exists xEx$. But this is inconsistent with an instance of Weak Existential Grounding (namely $E[\exists xEx] \leqslant \exists xEx$).

For the purpose of mimicking Krämer's argument, Fritz takes $T$ to be $\lambda p.p$.[62] Since $T(ET)$ then says that it is the case that something is the case (or something like that), it can safely be taken to be true and so from $(\exists Q^+)$ one can infer:

$(\exists Q^{++})$ $\lambda p.p(E\lambda p.p) < E\lambda p.p$.

This is not a counterexample to the irreflexivity of $<$. We do get a counterexample to a standard structural principle for $<$ if we assume either $\lambda p.p(E\lambda p.p) \doteq E\lambda p.p$, where $\doteq$ is akin to standard identity but of the appropriate grammatical type, or $E\lambda p.p < \lambda p.p(E\lambda p.p)$. In the first case, $E\lambda p.p < E\lambda p.p$ can be inferred from $(\exists Q^{++})$ – a violation of the irreflexivity of $<$. (It is here assumed that the relevant context is not 'opaque', i.e., that one can apply Leibniz's Law for $\doteq$ in the suggested way.) In the second case, we have a violation of the asymmetry of $<$. $\lambda p.p(E\lambda p.p) \doteq E\lambda p.p$ is a consequence of a principle known as $\beta$-conversion, and $E\lambda p.p < \lambda p.p(E\lambda p.p)$ a consequence of a principle Fritz calls '$\beta$-grounding', which is advocated by Fine (2012a). In his paper, Fritz sketches a general view on lambda abstraction that rejects both $\beta$-conversion and $\beta$-grounding.

Whether the view that Fritz sketches is viable or not, it can be argued that $(\exists Q)$ yields violations of structural principles about $<$ relative to *all* the impure logics that have been developed so far. Here are indeed two consequences of $(\exists Q^+)$:

(I) If $<$ is irreflexive, then there is no operator $T$ such that $T(ET)$ holds and the inference from $T\phi < \psi$ to $\phi < \psi$ is generally acceptable;
(II) If $<$ is asymmetric, then there is no operator $T$ such that $T(ET)$ holds and $\phi < T\phi$ generally holds.

All the impure logics of grounding that have been developed so far, at least all those I am aware of, are at odds either with the consequent of (I) or with the consequent of (II). Let for instance $T\phi$ be defined as $\neg\neg\phi$. $T(ET)$ then certainly holds. Some of the logics in question take $\neg\neg\phi$ to be ground-theoretically equivalent to $\phi$ – in which case they take the inference from $\neg\neg\phi < \psi$ to $\phi < \psi$ to be generally acceptable. This is the case, for instance, of the logic developed in Correia (2010) and of the logic determined by the semantics in Fine (2012a). All the other logics take $\phi < \neg\neg\phi$ to generally hold. This is the case, for instance, of the logic determined by the proof-theory in

---

[62] Another option, not considered by Fritz, would be to take $T$ to be a primitive truth operator. It would be interesting to see how Fritz's discussion could be supplemented if this option were also taken into account.

Fine (2012a), the logic developed in Correia (2017) and the one developed in deRosset and Fine (2023).

### 4.2.2 Fritz's Puzzles

Fritz (2022) presents two challenges for people taking the concept of *immediate* grounding to be meaningful, in the form of two arguments which show that given plausible assumptions about the notion, contradiction follows. The two arguments are similar, but one of them is significantly simpler and so I shall mainly focus on it.

The argument is formulated in a language with an operator $<$ for (factive) *immediate partial* grounding, sentential quantifiers which can bind singular variables ($p$, $q$, ...) as well as plural variables ($pp$, $qq$, ...), a symbol $\epsilon$ to express plurality membership, and a sentential operator $\bigwedge$ that takes a plural variable $pp$ to make the sentence $\bigwedge pp$, intended to express conjunction (of non-fixed arity).

Following Fritz, let me lay down the following definitions:

$Tpp := \forall p(p \in pp \supset p)$
$\overline{\forall} pp \phi := \forall pp(Tpp \supset \phi)$
$pp \doteq qq := \forall p(p \in pp \equiv p \in qq)$

The first argument consists in showing that the following two principles are inconsistent (here and below I use Fritz's labels):

$(\bigwedge <)$ $\overline{\forall} pp \forall p(p < \bigwedge pp \equiv p \in pp)$
$(\bigwedge T)$ $\forall pp(\bigwedge pp \equiv Tpp)$

From $(\bigwedge <)$ one can infer $(S\bigwedge)$ and from $(\bigwedge T)$ $(T\bigwedge)$:

$(S\bigwedge)$ $\overline{\forall} pp \overline{\forall} qq(\bigwedge pp = \bigwedge qq \supset pp \doteq qq)$
$(T\bigwedge)$ $\overline{\forall} pp \bigwedge pp$

Now these two principles yield a violation of a higher-order version of a corollary of Cantor's theorem. Cantor's theorem says that given any set $E$, there is no *surjective* function from $E$ to its power set $\mathcal{P}(E)$. The corollary in question says that given any set $E$, there is no *total injective* function from $\mathcal{P}(E)$ to $E$. What the two principles say, in set-theoretic idiom, is that $\bigwedge$ is a total injective function from the power set of the set of all truths to the set of all truths – in direct violation of the corollary of Cantor's theorem. A version of this corollary can be established in a suitable higher-order language. Hence the inconsistency of $(S\bigwedge)$ and $(T\bigwedge)$.

($\wedge T$) looks harmless, as it seems to simply record the behaviour of conjunctions relative to the notion of 'being the case'. ($\wedge <$) is the specific ground-theoretic source of the inconsistency. What could be said in its favour?

It is true that one sometimes hears or reads statements like 'what immediately (strictly fully) grounds a conjunctive fact are its conjuncts taken together', and that prima facie there seems to be some truth that these statements express. Granted that an immediate partial ground is just a part of an immediate strict full ground, the above statement entails 'what immediately partially grounds a conjunctive fact are its conjuncts taken separately'. ($\wedge <$) looks like a very good way of formalizing a generalization of the latter statement.

But in order to assess ($\wedge <$) seriously more than first impressions about a notion are needed. I will not go through a detailed discussion here, but I would simply like to point out that according to some of the conceptions of grounding that have been discussed in Section 3, whatever immediate partial grounding may turn out to be, ($\wedge <$) must clearly be rejected.

I have in mind the worldly conceptions of grounding at work in Correia (2010), Fine (2012a)-semantic side, Lovett (2020a) and Correia (2023). Let me simply focus on Fine (2012a) for illustration. In order to stick to the Finean talk of facts (or proposition or contents) and their ground-theoretic connections at the semantic level, I will interpret the quantifiers in ($\wedge <$) not as sentential quantifiers, but as nominal quantifiers ranging over such entities. The following considerations could be made thoroughly higher-order.

Let $s$ and $t$ be two states such that $t$ is not a part of $s$, and consider the distinct facts $F = \{s, st\}$ and $G = \{s\}$, which we suppose obtain. (Here and in the next argument, I use '$st$' for the fusion of $s$ and $t$.) By ($\wedge <$) 'right-to-left', $F$ should be an immediate partial ground of the conjunction $F \sqcap G$ of $F$ and $G$. But it turns out that $F \sqcap G = F$, and I guess that, whatever immediate partial grounding may turn out to be, we do not want to say that $F$ is an immediate partial ground of itself.[63]

Here is a stronger argument against ($\wedge <$), one which does not rely on considerations of self-grounding. Consider three states $s$, $t$ and $u$ that are disjoint (not just distinct) from one another. Consider then the three facts $F = \{s\}$, $G = \{t\}$ and $H = \{u\}$, which we suppose obtain. By ($\wedge <$) 'right-to-left', $F$ immediately partially grounds $F \sqcap (G \sqcap H)$.[64] Since $F \sqcap (G \sqcap H) = (F \sqcap G) \sqcap H$, ($\wedge <$)

---

[63] Some might wish to reject ($\wedge <$) 'right-to-left' either on the grounds that conjunction must always operate on at least *two* facts or on the grounds that degenerate conjunctions of one fact are not immediately partially grounded in the corresponding fact. It is in order to avoid such issues that I chose $F$ and $G$ distinct in this argument.

[64] Note that given the initial mereological assumption, $F$ and $G \sqcap H$ are distinct. The issues mentioned in the previous footnote are thus also avoided in the present argument.

'left-to-right' allows one to infer that either $F = F \sqcap G$ or $F = H$. But this requires that either $s = st$ or $s = u$, and this is ruled out by our initial mereological assumption.

The more complex argument put forward by Fritz is also ineffective if the conceptions of grounding under consideration above are taken for granted. In place of $(\wedge<)$, it invokes three similar principles: the immediate partial grounds of a true binary conjunction are its conjuncts; every true binary disjunction has at least one disjunct as an immediate partial ground, and every immediate partial ground of a disjunction is one of the disjuncts; every true universal quantification has all its instances as immediate partial grounds, and every immediate partial ground of a universal quantification is either one of its instances or a suitable 'totality fact'. The previous objections against $(\wedge<)$ also apply to the first principle, since these arguments invoked specifically binary conjunctions. Similar objections can be formulated against the other two principles.

### 4.2.3 Wilhelm's Inconsistency

Wilhelm (2021) shows that the following principles are inconsistent, where $<$ stands for (factive) immediate partial grounding and $\approx$ stands for propositional identity:

(1) $\phi < (\psi \wedge \chi)$ iff $(\psi \wedge \chi)$ and $(\phi \approx \psi$ or $\phi \approx \chi)$;

(2) $\phi < \neg(\psi \wedge \chi)$ iff $\phi$ and $(\phi \approx \neg\psi$ or $\phi \approx \neg\chi)$;

(3) $\phi < \psi \vee \chi$ iff $\phi$ and $(\phi \approx \psi$ or $\phi \approx \chi)$;

(4) $\phi < \neg(\psi \vee \chi)$ iff $\neg(\psi \vee \chi)$ and $(\phi \approx \neg\psi$ or $\phi \approx \neg\chi)$;

(5) $\phi < \neg\neg\psi$ iff $\phi$ and $\phi \approx \psi$;

(6) Sometimes, $\phi$ but not $\phi < \phi$;

(7) $(\phi \wedge \psi) \approx \neg(\neg\phi \vee \neg\psi)$.

And he also shows that the inconsistency remains if (7) is replaced by:

(8) $(\phi \vee \psi) \approx \neg(\neg\phi \wedge \neg\psi)$.

Why should these facts be important? Because, Wilhelm suggests, (1)–(5) are – I quote – 'standard conditions for immediate partial grounding' and (7) and (8) are 'standard identity conditions for propositions'. (He does not claim that (6) is also a 'standard condition', but it seems clear that he thinks so.)

I grant that (1)–(5) have some intuitive pull (see my comments on $(\wedge<)$ in the discussion of Fritz's puzzles above). But I am not sure they are *standard*.

Wilhelm mentions Fine (2012a), Correia (2017) and Krämer (2018) as evidence that they are. Fine (2012a) explicitly talks about immediate grounding, and some of the things he says about it suggest indeed a picture on which (1)–(5) hold. By contrast, neither Correia (2017) nor Krämer (2018) talks about immediate grounding at all, and so it is tempting to think that they provide no evidence for Wilhelm's claim. However, the logics in Correia (2017) and Krämer (2018) validate Fine's (2012a) elimination rules for strict full grounding (see Figure 10), and we may charitably grant that these may be seen as vindicating, modulo a proper definition of immediate partial grounding, the principles under consideration.

Be that as it may, no one in the literature is vulnerable to Wilhelm's attack. He says that (7) and (8) are standard identity conditions for propositions, but he does not give references to back his claim. Now, and that is what is important, none of those who can be seen as endorsing (1)–(5) has also endorsed (7) and (8). Take the papers mentioned in the previous paragraph. Correia (2017) has a theory featuring the operator $\approx$, which is there taken to express identity between propositions. But the theory does not validate (7) and (8). Worse, on that theory, $(\phi \wedge \psi) \approx \neg(\neg\phi \vee \neg\psi)$ and $(\phi \vee \psi) \approx \neg(\neg\phi \wedge \neg\psi)$ *never* hold. Krämer 2018 also has the operator $\approx$, taken to express sameness of content, but on his view $(\phi \wedge \psi) \approx \neg(\neg\phi \vee \neg\psi)$ and $(\phi \vee \psi) \approx \neg(\neg\phi \wedge \neg\psi)$ also never hold. If $\approx$ is understood as implying ground-theoretic equivalence, then on Fine's (2021a) proof-theoretic account of grounding, $(\phi \wedge \psi) \approx \neg(\neg\phi \vee \neg\psi)$ must fail since $\phi \wedge \psi$ and $\neg(\neg\phi \vee \neg\psi)$ do not have the same strict full grounds; and for the same reason, $(\phi \vee \psi) \approx \neg(\neg\phi \wedge \neg\psi)$ must also fail.

Of course, (7) and (8) *are* validated in some logics – for instance in the logic advocated in Correia (2010) and in the logic determined by Fine's (2012a) semantics given that $\approx$ is interpreted as factual identity. But as I argued in the previous section, these logics are at odds with (1), and they can be shown to be at odds with (2)–(5) in much the same way.

Thus we see that Wilhelm invokes mixed principles about grounding and propositional identity that belong to quite different general conceptions of these notions. It is therefore not surprising that the mix ends up being inconsistent.[65]

---

[65] Litland's (2021) two theories of propositional identity I alluded to in footnote 51 connect propositional identity with immediate grounding. They both validate (1)–(4); one of them validates (5) but invalidates (7) and (8); the other one invalidates (5) but validates (7) and (8). On Poggiolesi's (2023) account, (1), (3) and (5) are validated, (2), (4), (7) and (8) are not – although some principles in the vicinity are validated. I lack space to properly discuss these views.

# Appendix: Labelled Trees

Labelled trees have often been invoked in this Element. In this appendix, I define them and introduce other tree-theoretic notions that I have used at various places.

I start off by defining *trees*[66]:

**Definition** (Tree). *A tree is a pair $\langle N, \sqsubset \rangle$ where N (the nodes of the tree) is a non-empty set and $\sqsubset$ (the precedence relation of the tree) is a strict partial order on N such that the following two conditions are satisfied:*

1. *For all $n \in N$, the set of predecessors of n in the structure – namely, $\{m \in N : m \sqsubset n\}$ – is finite and totally ordered by $\sqsubset$;*
2. *N has a unique minimal element for $\sqsubset$.*

Given a tree $\langle N, \sqsubset \rangle$, I adopt the following standard definitions:

- The *root* is the unique minimal element for $\sqsubset$ in $N$;
- A *leaf* is a node that has no successor for $\sqsubset$ in $N$;
- A *parent* of a node $n$ is a node that immediately precedes $n$, that is, a node $m$ such that $m \sqsubset n$ and there is no node $l$ such that $m \sqsubset l$ and $l \sqsubset n$;
- A *child* of a node $n$ is a node that immediately succeeds $n$, that is, a node $m$ such that $n \sqsubset m$ and there is no node $l$ such that $n \sqsubset l$ and $l \sqsubset m$;
- A *branch* is a set of nodes totally ordered by $\sqsubset$ that is not strictly contained in another such set of nodes.

Of course, a node $n$ is a parent of a node $m$ iff $m$ is a child of $n$. Whereas a node can have more than one child, a node cannot have more than one parent. Every node distinct from a leaf has children, and every node distinct from the root has a parent.[67]

Let the *length* of a branch $B$ of a tree be the order type of $\langle B, \sqsubset \rangle$, that is, the ordinal number which is order-isomorphic to it. A branch can have any length from 1 to $\omega$ included. The *height* of a tree is defined to be (i) the length of its

---

[66] The second condition, which guarantees that the trees so defined are 'rooted', is in some contexts considered to be optional. The standard definitions of trees / rooted trees one encounters in set theory are more general: condition 1 below is replaced by the weaker condition that the set of predecessors of any node is well-ordered by $\sqsubset$ (see for instance Jech 2002: 114). Rooted trees in this general sense that are not trees in the sense I introduce here are too 'high' for the applications I have been concerned with in this Element.

[67] The first claim generally holds of trees as standardly defined in set theory (see footnote 66), but the second claim does not: for instance, in the tree whose nodes are the ordinals $\leq \omega$ and whose precedence relation is the standard order over the ordinals, $\omega$ does not have a parent.

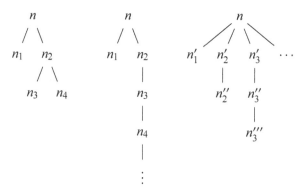

**Figure A.1** Finite and infinite heights

longest branch(es) if all the branches of the tree have a finite length and there is indeed a longest branch, (ii) $\omega$ otherwise. In Figure A.1, the tree on the left has height 3 and the other two trees have height $\omega$ – the one in the middle because it has a branch of infinite length, the one on the right because it has only finite branches but no longest branch.

**Definition** (Subtree). *Let $T = \langle N, \sqsubset \rangle$ be a tree and let $n \in N$. A subtree of $T$ from node $n$ is any pair $\langle N^*, \sqsubset^* \rangle$ that satisfies the following conditions:*

1. $n \in N^*$;
2. For all $m \in N^*$ such that $m \neq n$, $n \sqsubset m$ (hence, $N^* \subseteq N$);
3. For all $m, l \in N$ such that $n \sqsubset m$, $m \sqsubset l$ and $l \in N^*$, $m \in N^*$;
4. $\sqsubset^*$ is $\sqsubset$'s restriction to $N^*$.

As one can readily verify, if $T^*$ is a subtree of a given tree $T$ from a node $n$, then $T^*$ is itself a tree and its root is $n$.

Let $T = \langle N, \sqsubset \rangle$ be a tree. We adopt the following definitions:

- A subtree $\langle N^*, \sqsubset^* \rangle$ of $T$ is said to be *regular* iff for any $n \in N$ such that some $\sqsubset$-child of $n$ is in $N^*$, all of $n$'s $\sqsubset$-children are in $N^*$;
- An *initial subtree* of $T$ is a regular subtree of $T$ from $T$'s root;
- A subtree $\langle N^*, \sqsubset^* \rangle$ of $T$ from $n \in N$ is said to be *final* iff $N^* = \{m \in N : n \sqsubset m\}$.

Note that given any tree and any node $n$ of the tree, there is one, and only one, final subtree of the tree from $n$. Also note that every final subtree is regular. In Figure A.2, $T_1$ is a non-regular subtree of $U$, $T_2$ is an initial subtree of $U$, and $T_3$ is a final subtree of $U$ from node $n_2$.

Appendix 81

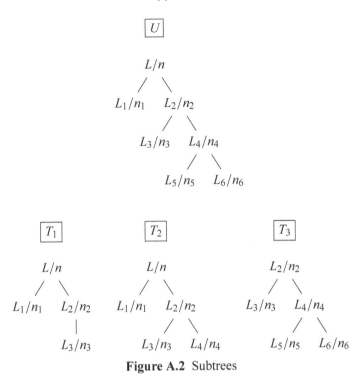

**Figure A.2** Subtrees

**Definition** (Labelled tree). *A* labelled tree *is a triple* $\langle N, \sqsubset, \ell \rangle$, *where* $\langle N, \sqsubset \rangle$ *is a tree and* $\ell$ *(the* labelling *function) a function that assigns to each element of N a given entity.*

The output of a labelling function for a given node is said to *label* or to *occupy* the node. The label that occupies the root of a labelled tree is called its *bottom*, and the set of labels that occupy its leaves is called its *top*.

We define *subtrees of labelled trees* in the obvious way:

**Definition** (Subtree of a labelled tree). *Let* $T = \langle N, \sqsubset, \ell \rangle$ *be a labelled tree and let* $n \in N$. *A subtree of T from node n is any triple* $\langle N^*, \sqsubset^*, \ell^* \rangle$, *where* $\langle N^*, \sqsubset^* \rangle$ *is a subtree of* $\langle N, \sqsubset \rangle$ *from n and* $\ell^*$ *is* $\ell$ *'s restriction to* $N^*$.

Subtrees of labelled trees are of course themselves labelled trees. The definitions of regular / initial / final subtrees are also extended in the obvious way. Let $T = \langle N, \sqsubset, \ell \rangle$ be a labelled tree. We put:

- A subtree $\langle N^*, \sqsubset^*, \ell^* \rangle$ of $T$ is *regular* iff $\langle N^*, \sqsubset^* \rangle$ is a regular subtree of $\langle N, \sqsubset \rangle$;

- An *initial subtree* of $T$ is a regular subtree of $T$ from $T$'s root;
- A subtree $\langle N^*, \sqsubset^*, \ell^* \rangle$ of $T$ from $n \in N$ is said to be *final* iff $\langle N^*, \sqsubset^* \rangle$ is a final subtree of $\langle N, \sqsubset \rangle$.

I close this appendix by one last definition: an *isomorphism from labelled tree* $\langle N, \sqsubset, \ell \rangle$ *to labelled tree* $\langle N^*, \sqsubset^*, \ell^* \rangle$ is an isomorphism (in the usual sense) $f$ from $\langle N, \sqsubset \rangle$ to $\langle N^*, \sqsubset^* \rangle$ such that $\ell(n) = \ell^*(f(n))$ for all $n \in N$.

# References

Anderson, A. R. and Belnap, N. D. 1962. Tautological Entailments, *Philosophical Studies*, 13, 9–24.

Anderson, A. R. and Belnap, N. D. 1963. First-Degree Entailments, *Math. Annalen*, 149, 302–19.

Angell, R. B. 1977. Three Systems of First Degree Entailment, *Journal of Symbolic Logic*, 42, 147.

— 1989. Deducibility, Entailment and Analytic Containment, in J. Norman and R. Sylvan (eds.), *Directions in Relevant Logic*, Dordrecht: Kluwer Academic, 119–43.

Batchelor, R. 2010. Grounds and Consequences, *Grazer Philosophische Studien*, 80, 65–77.

Bennett, K. 2011. By Our Bootstraps, *Philosophical Perspectives*, 25(1), 27–41.

— 2017. *Making Things up*, Oxford: Oxford University Press.

Bolzano, B. 1837. *Wissenschaftslehre*, Sulzbach: Seidel.

Brenner, A., Maurin, A.-S., Skiles, A., Stenwall, R. and Thompson, N. 2021. Metaphysical Explanation, in E. N. Zalta (ed.), *The Stanford Encyclopedia of Philosophy* (Winter 2021 ed.), https://plato.stanford.edu/cgi-bin/encyclopedia/archinfo.cgi?entry=metaphysical-explanation.

Correia, F. 2005. *Existential Dependence and Cognate Notions*, Munich: Philosophia.

— 2010. Grounding and Truth-Functions, *Logique et Analyse*, 53(211), 251–79.

— 2011. From Grounding to Truth-Making: Some Thoughts, in A. Reboul (ed.), *Philosophical Papers Dedicated to Kevin Mulligan*, Genève. https://.unige.ch/lettres/philo/mulligan/festschrift/. Reprinted in A. Reboul (ed.), *Mind, Values, and Metaphysics: Philosophical Essays in Honor of Kevin Mulligan*, Vol. I, 2014, Cham: Springer, 85–98.

— 2014. Logical Grounds, *Review of Symbolic Logic*, 7(1), 31–59.

— 2015. Logical Grounding and First-Degree Entailments, in S. Lapointe (ed.), *Themes from Ontology, Mind, and Logic: Present and Past - Essays in Honour of Peter Simons*, Grazer Philosophische Studien, Vol, Leiden: Brill Rodopi, 3–15.

— 2016. On the Logic of Factual Equivalence, *Review of Symbolic Logic*, 9(1), 103–22.

— 2017. An Impure Logic of Representational Grounding, *Journal of Philosophical Logic*, 46(5), 507–38.

— 2020. Granularity, in M. Raven (ed.), *Routledge Handbook of Metaphysical Grounding*, New York: Routledge, 228–43.

— 2021a. Fundamentality from Grounding Trees, *Synthese*, 199, 5965–94.

— 2021b. The Logic of Relative Fundamentality, *Synthese*, 198, 1279–301.

— 2023. A New Semantic Framework for the Logic of Worldly Grounding (and beyond), in F. Faroldi and F. Van De Putte (eds.), *Kit Fine on Truthmakers, Relevance, and Non-Classical Logic*, Outstanding Contributions to Logic, Vol 26, Cham: Springer, 573–600.

Correia, F. and Skiles, A. 2019. Grounding, Essence, and Identity, *Philosophy and Phenomenological Research*, 98(3), 642–70.

Dasgupta, S. 2014. On the Plurality of Grounds, *Philosophers' Imprint*, 14(20), 1–28.

deRosset, L. 2013a. What is Weak Ground?, *Essays in Philosophy*, 14(1), 7–18.

— 2013b. Grounding Explanations, *Philosophers' Imprint*, 13(7), 1–26.

— 2014. On Weak Ground, *Review of Symbolic Logic*, 7(4), 713–44.

— 2015. Better Semantics for the Pure Logic of Ground, *Analytic Philosophy*, 56(3), 229–52.

deRosset, L. and Fine, K. 2023. A Semantics for the Impure Logic of Ground, *Journal of Philosophical Logic*, 52, 415–93.

Donaldson, T. 2017. The (Metaphysical) Foundations of Arithmetic?, *Noûs*, 51(4), 775–801.

Fine K. 2001. The Question of Realism, *Philosophers' Imprint*, 1(1), 1–30.

— 2010. Some Puzzles of Ground, *Notre Dame Journal of Formal Logic*, 51(1), 97–118.

— 2012a. Guide to Ground, in F. Correia and B. Schneider (eds.), *Metaphysical Grounding: Understanding the Structure of Reality*, Cambridge: Cambridge University Press, 37–80.

— 2012b. The Pure Logic of Ground, *Review of Symbolic Logic*, 25(1), 1–25.

— 2016. Angellic Content, *Journal of Philosophical Logic*, 45, 199–226.

— 2017a. Truthmaker Semantics, in B. Hale, C. Wright and A. Miller (eds.), *A Companion to the Philosophy of Language*, 2nd ed., Chichester, West Sussex: Wiley Blackwell, 556–77.

— 2017b. A Theory of Truthmaker Content I: Conjunction, Disjunction and Negation, *Journal of Philosophical Logic*, 46(6), 625–74.

— 2017c. A Theory of Truthmaker Content II: Subject-Matter, Common Content, Remainder and Ground, *Journal of Philosophical Logic*, 46(6), 675–702.

— 2023. The Algebraic and Structural Approaches to Truthmaker Semantics: Response to Fabrice Correia, in F. Faroldi and F. Van De Putte (eds.), *Kit Fine on Truthmakers, Relevance, and Non-Classical Logic*, Outstanding Contributions to Logic, Vol 26, Cham: Springer, 2023, 601–13.

Fritz, P. 2020. On Higher-Order Logical Grounds, *Analysis*, 80(4), 656–66.

— 2022. Ground and Grain, *Philosophy and Phenomenological Research*, 105(2), 299–330.

Halbach, V. 2011. *Axiomatic Theories of Truth*, Cambridge: Cambridge University Press.

Jech, T. 2002. *Set Theory*, Berlin: Springer.

Korbmacher, J. 2018a. Axiomatic Theories of Partial Ground I: The Base Theory, *Journal of Philosophical Logic*, 47(2), 161–91.

— 2018b. Axiomatic Theories of Partial Ground II: Partial Ground and Typed Truth, *Journal of Philosophical Logic*, 47(2), 193–226.

Krämer, S. 2013. A Simpler Puzzle of Ground, *Thought*, 2(2), 85–9.

— 2018. Towards a Theory of Ground-Theoretic Content, *Synthese*, 195, 785–814.

— 2020. Puzzles, in M. Raven (ed.), *Routledge Handbook of Metaphysical Grounding*, New York: Routledge, 271–82.

— 2021. Ground-Theoretic Equivalence, *Synthese*, 198(2),1643–83.

Krämer, S. and Roski, S. 2015. A Note on the Logic of Worldly Ground, *Thought: A Journal of Philosophy*, 4(1), 59–68.

Kripke, S. 1975. Outline of a Theory of Truth, *Journal of Philosophy*, 72, 690–716.

Leuenberger, S. 2014. Grounding and Necessity, *Inquiry*, 57(2), 151–74.

Litland, J. 2015. Grounding, Explanation, and the Limit of Internality, *Philosophical Review*, 124(4), 481–532.

— 2016. Pure Logic of Many-Many Ground, *Journal of Philosophical Logic*, 45(5), 531–77.

— 2017. Grounding Ground, *Oxford Studies in Metaphysics*, 10, 279–316.

— 2018a. Bicollective Ground: Towards a (Hyper)graphic Account, in R. Bliss and G. Priest (eds.), *Reality and Its Structure*, Oxford: Oxford University Press, 140–64.

— 2018b. Pure Logic of Iterated Full Ground, *Review of Symbolic Logic*, 11(3), 411–35.

— 2021. A Note on the Wilhelmine Inconsistency, *Analysis*, 81(4), 639–47.

Lovett, A. 2020a. The Logic of Ground, *Journal of Philosophical Logic*, 49, 13–49.

— 2020b. The Puzzles of Ground, *Philosophical Studies*, 177, 2541–64.

Poggiolesi, F. 2016. On Defining the Notion of Complete and Immediate Formal Grounding, *Synthese*, 193(1), 3147–67.

— 2018. On Constructing a Logic for the Notion of Complete and Immediate Formal Grounding, *Synthese*, 195(2), 1231–54.

— 2023. Grounding and Propositional Identity: A Solution to Wilhelm's Inconsistencies, *Logic and Logical Philosophy*, 32, 33–38.

Raven, M. 2015. Ground, *Philosophy Compass*, 10, 322–33.

— (ed.) 2020. *Routledge Handbook of Metaphysical Grounding*, New York: Routledge.

Rosen, G. 2010. Metaphysical Dependence: Grounding and Reduction, in B. Hale and A. Hoffmann (eds.), *Modality: Metaphysics, Logic, and Epistemology*, Oxford: Oxford University Press, 109–36.

Roski, S. and Schnieder, B. (eds.) 2022. *Bolzano's Philosophy of Grounding: Translations and Studies*, Oxford: Oxford University Press.

Schaffer, J. 2009. On What Grounds What, in D. Manley, D. J. Chalmers and R. Wasserman (eds.), *Metametaphysics: New Essays on the Foundations of Ontology*, Oxford: Oxford University Press, 347–83.

— 2010. Monism: The Priority of the Whole, *Philosophical Review*, 119(1), 31–76.

Schaffer, J. 2012. Grounding, Transitivity, and Contrastivity, in F. Correia and B. Schnieder (eds.), *Metaphysical Grounding: Understanding the Structure of Reality*, Cambridge: Cambridge University, 122–38.

Schnieder, B. 2010. A Puzzle about 'Because', *Logique & Analyse*, 53(211), 317–43.

— 2011. A Logic for 'Because', *Review of Symbolic Logic*, 4(3), 445–65.

Shumener, E. 2020. Identity, in M. Raven (ed.), *Routledge Handbook of Metaphysical Grounding*, New York: Routledge, 413–24.

Skiles, A. 2015. Against Grounding Necessitarianism, *Erkenntnis*, 80(4), 717–51.

Wilhelm, I. 2021. Grounding and Propositional Identity, *Analysis*, 81(1), 80–1.

Woods, J. 2018. Emptying a Paradox of Ground, *Journal of Philosophical Logic*, 47, 631–48.

# Acknowledgements

I am grateful to the editors, Brad Armour-Garb and Fred Kroon, for their constant support, and to two anonymous reviewers and Lisa Vogt for helpful comments on a first draft. Work on the Element was supported by the Swiss National Science Foundation, project 100012_197172.

# Philosophy and Logic

## Bradley Armour-Garb
*SUNY Albany*

Bradley Armour-Garb is chair and Professor of Philosophy at SUNY Albany. His books include *The Law of Non-Contradiction* (co-edited with Graham Priest and J. C. Beall, 2004), *Deflationary Truth* and *Deflationism and Paradox* (both co-edited with J. C. Beall, 2005), *Pretense and Pathology* (with James Woodbridge, Cambridge University Press, 2015), *Reflections on the Liar* (2017), and *Fictionalism in Philosophy* (co-edited with Fred Kroon, 2020).

## Frederick Kroon
*The University of Auckland*

Frederick Kroon is Emeritus Professor of Philosophy at the University of Auckland. He has authored numerous papers in formal and philosophical logic, ethics, philosophy of language, and metaphysics, and is the author of *A Critical Introduction to Fictionalism* (with Stuart Brock and Jonathan McKeown-Green, 2018).

### About the Series

This Cambridge Elements series provides an extensive overview of the many and varied connections between philosophy and logic. Distinguished authors provide an up-to-date summary of the results of current research in their fields and give their own take on what they believe are the most significant debates influencing research, drawing original conclusions.

# Cambridge Elements

# Philosophy and Logic

## Elements in the Series

*Higher-Order Logic and Type Theory*
John L. Bell

*Proofs and Models in Philosophical Logic*
Greg Restall

*Gödel's Incompleteness Theorems*
Juliette Kennedy

*Classical First-Order Logic*
Stewart Shapiro and Teresa Kouri Kissel

*Logical Consequence*
Gila Sher

*Temporal Logics*
Valentin Goranko

*The Many Faces of Impossibility*
Koji Tanaka and Alexander Sandgren

*Relevance Logic*
Shay Allen Logan

*Propositional Quantifiers*
Peter Fritz

*Logic and Information*
Edwin Mares

*Meinongianism*
Maria Elisabeth Reicher

*The Logic of Grounding*
Fabrice Correia

A full series listing is available at: www.cambridge.org/EPL

Printed by Integrated Books International,
United States of America